Pop-Up Retail

Ephemeral stores, also known as pop-up stores, have existed since the beginning of trade between consumers. They appeared in city centres, villages or other convenient places where they proposed an offering and then disappeared as soon as its offering was wearied. This is a very similar experience to the current phenomenon; ephemeral stores appear unannounced and disappear without notice or can morph into something else. Brands adopt these stores because of the array of benefits they present and their characterizing features. Consumers, on the other hand, are not only positively reactive to ephemeral stores, they actively demand these novel, engaging, satisfying or beneficial stores more than ever as they provide them with constant change and surprise.

Focusing on ephemeral retailing, this book aims to provide a clear understanding of what it is, how it developed and why it gained importance in today's busy retail scene. As many brands are adopting ephemeral stores into their distribution channels or using them as unique touchpoints, this book proposes a categorization of ephemeral retailing, explaining different ephemeral store vocations based on different brand strategies and objectives. With many professional opinions about ephemeral stores and a body of academic research developing, this book aims to combine all knowledge about the topic into one concise publication: it clarifies, consolidates and creates a clear understanding about the topic of ephemeral retailing that will inform future research and activity.

The book is written for academics, students and retail professionals with an interest in relevant fields such as retail marketing and management, brand management and distribution.

Ghalia Boustani is a researcher at Paris 1 Panthéon Sorbonne and holds a Doctorate degree from Ecole Supérieure des affaires. Her main research interest is in ephemeral retailing; she has developed her first research on pop-up stores in the Middle East and now is focusing her research on studying pop-up stores in Europe.

Routledge Focus on Business and Management

The fields of business and management have grown exponentially as areas of research and education. This growth presents challenges for readers trying to keep up with the latest important insights. *Routledge Focus on Business and Management* presents small books on big topics and how they intersect with the world of business.

Individually, each title in the series provides coverage of a key academic topic, whilst collectively, the series forms a comprehensive collection across the business disciplines.

How to Resolve Conflict in Organizations
The Power of People Models and Procedure
Annamaria Garden

Trade Governance of the Belt and Road Initiative
Economic Logic, Value Choices, and Institutional Arrangement
Dawei Cheng

The Innovative Business School
Mentoring Today's Leaders for Tomorrow's Global Challenges
Edited by Daphne Halkias, Michael Neubert, Paul W. Thurman, Chris Adendorff and Sameh Abadir

Pop-Up Retail
The Evolution, Application and Future of Ephemeral Stores
Ghalia Boustani

For more information about this series, please visit: www.routledge.com/Routledge-Focus-on-Business-and-Management/book-series/FBM

Pop-Up Retail

The Evolution, Application and
Future of Ephemeral Stores

Ghalia Boustani

Routledge
Taylor & Francis Group

LONDON AND NEW YORK

First published 2021
by Routledge
2 Park Square, Milton Park, Abingdon, Oxon OX14 4RN

and by Routledge
605 Third Avenue, New York, NY 10158

Routledge is an imprint of the Taylor & Francis Group, an informa business

© 2021 Ghalia Boustani

The right of Ghalia Boustani to be identified as author of this work
has been asserted by her in accordance with sections 77 and 78 of
the Copyright, Designs and Patents Act 1988.

British Library Cataloguing-in-Publication Data
A catalogue record for this book is available from the British Library

Library of Congress Cataloging-in-Publication Data
Names: Boustani, Ghalia, author.
Title: Pop-up retail: the evolution, application and future of
ephemeral stores / Ghalia Boustani.
Description: Abingdon, Oxon; New York, NY: Routledge, 2021. |
Series: Routledge focus on business & management |
Includes bibliographical references and index.
Identifiers: LCCN 2021006549 (print) | LCCN 2021006550 (ebook) |
ISBN 9780367628529 (hbk) | ISBN 9780367628550 (pbk) |
ISBN 9781003111092 (ebk)
Subjects: LCSH: Stores, Retail. | Retail trade. | New business
enterprises.
Classification: LCC HF5429.B6225 2021 (print) | LCC HF5429
(ebook) | DDC381/.1—dc23
LC record available at https://lccn.loc.gov/2021006549
LC ebook record available at https://lccn.loc.gov/2021006550

ISBN: 978-0-367-62852-9 (hbk)
ISBN: 978-0-367-62855-0 (pbk)
ISBN: 978-1-003-11109-2 (ebk)

Typeset in Times New Roman
by codeMantra

"We rarely understand the meaning or value of time.
We seek to quantify it,
We wish we can get hold of it,
We hope to contain it,
But only realize that time is out of our hands and far from our reach.
All we can do is live the moment, as this moment is the only version of what time can look like"
Chawki, I dedicate this work to you.

Contents

About the author   ix
Acknowledgements   xi

Introduction   1

1 From retail to ephemeral retail   10

2 What are ephemeral stores and how can we
   define them?   36

3 Somewhere between communications and
   distributions: categorizing ephemeral stores   57

4 Understanding the future by looking
   at the past   78

   Conclusion   112

   Index   133

About the author

Ghalia Boustani is a researcher at Paris 1 Panthéon Sorbonne and holds a Doctorate degree from Ecole Supérieure des affaires. Her main research interest is in ephemeral retailing; she has developed her first research on pop-up stores in the Middle East and now is focusing her research on studying pop-up stores in Europe. She has published "Ephemeral Retailing: Pop-up stores in a Postmodern consumption era" and presented her research in different marketing and retailing colloquy. Throughout her academic journey, she has also worked closely with professionals and entrepreneurs on several projects that have added value to her researches and developed a considerable amount of online content that looks at retailing in general and ephemeral retailing in particular.

Acknowledgements

I am grateful to all those who contributed in the making of this book, who believed in me and who believed that ephemeral retailing is a topic that should be acquiring more shelf space!

Despite the difficult days of 2020, it was important to keep working and moving forward. I remember how this book's proposal flourished around the spring term and the support it got from the Routledge team. With *Pop-up Retail: The Evolution, Application and Future of Ephemeral Stores*, I hope to bring more to the literature on pop-up stores and ephemeral retailing.

Along the way, and during the process of writing, many colleagues have provided generous comments and valuable feedback and proposed suggestions that were carefully considered in this manuscript.

We all grow to build our knowledge and refine it; I have done so with the guidance and support of my tutors and advisors. A special thanks to everyone who inspired me, accompanied me and contributed in making this book happen.

Introduction

Why academic research is paying closer attention to ephemeral stores?

London, Milan, New York or Paris; pop-up stores settle in large capitals and adapt to key seasons such as the end of year celebrations or "fashion weeks" to present innovative concepts by adopting different formats available. Luxury brands such as Colette, Stella McCartney or Hermès have been present in Milan, London or Paris for a limited time to present collections or selections of unique pieces or to make their collections accessible to the general public (Jones et al., 2017). These brands have also chosen strategic locations or innovative formats when they appear – highly theatrical vacant stores, showrooms or travelling formats such as London buses (De Lassus, 2012).

Several studies have focused on the Italian (Russo Spena et al., 2012) (Pomodoro, 2013), English (Jones et al., 2017; Taube & Warnaby, 2017; Klein et al., 2016), American (Niehm et al., 2007; Fowler & Bridges, 2010), French (De Lassus, 2012; Picot-Coupey, 2012; Picot-Coupey, 2014) or Taiwanese context to study pop-up stores from a brand or a customer perspective (Chen & Fiore, 2017). The wave of pop-up store adoption in Asian markets (Chen & Fiore, 2017), the Gulf and the Middle East (Boustani, 2020) took off only timidly and manifested later with greater magnitude after 2014. If pop-up stores were looking for new places to establish themselves, why is it that their adoption is increasing in less privileged places? And why are they still not formally acknowledged as distribution channels in their own right?

Several reasons have led researchers to study different angles regarding pop-up stores or to study pop-up store practices in different countries. Some studies were interested in looking at how pop-up stores contributed to the revitalization of city centres (Jones et al.,

2017). Research developed in the Taiwanese market, for instance, has looked at the desired benefits affecting consumer attitude and the consequent influence of attitude on behavioural intentions towards pop-up stores (Chen & Fiore, 2017). Researchers explored in other studies how brand-consumer interaction in pop-up stores can influence consumers' perception of luxury fashion retailers (Taube & Warnaby, 2017). In the context of luxury retail, studies examine the effectiveness of pop-up stores offering brand experiences while reaching out to existing and new target groups, to confront the risk of being seen as outdated and obsolete (Klein et al., 2016). Finally, some research aimed to explore the relationships between consumer innovation; market mavenism; the pleasure of shopping; and the beliefs, attitude and intentions of favouritism towards pop-up retail sales (Kim et al., 2010).

An emphasis on studies focusing on the reasons for adopting or for choosing pop-up stores in local or international contexts, such as those conducted by Picot-Coupey (2012, 2014), shows how these stores are means of operating a brand outside its initial territory. Moreover, these studies show that pop-up stores help brands raise their international profile in a new foreign market. Pop-up stores were referred to as methods of distributing and communicating brands in international markets. These are ways to test a new store concept for an established retail brand and further expand the store network to open in the new market (Alexander et al., 2018).

Researchers presented three reasons for adopting pop-up stores as a fashion of operation outside the brand's local context. The first reason for adopting of ephemeral stores by established brands or young brands is to test their concepts with targeted consumers who are not yet familiar with them. The relatively low cost of a pop-up store allows the brand to "life-size" test the concept of understanding consumer preferences for this type and format of sale. They thus make it possible to assess the feasibility of future openings and help initiate the international development of a foreign brand. Pop-up stores are efficient ways to build and manage the brand image internationally.

The second motive helps anchor an international brand's status as being present in the most sought-after places; the "places to be". It is a kind of showroom that offers visibility to the brand at a lower cost than permanent stores. Three different approaches appear under this second motive. Pop-up stores are effective means to arouse influencer and consumer curiosity. They are also tools for creating a "buzz" that will generate brand dynamics. They educate foreign consumers and potential partners about the concept they are presenting. The pop-up store's extension abroad helps support brand awareness among staff, stakeholders and consumers. To conclude, the third motive seems motivated by the agility offered by this format. Through an ephemeral store, the brand is very responsive. It takes root in key locations at specific times of the year to be close to consumers. The brand comes in a "ready-to-use" format which allows it to generate profits to finance its overseas trips (Picot-Coupey, 2012).

Other studies looked at pop-up store adoption motives in the Middle Eastern market context to understand if brands operate differently than northern American or European markets. It was highlighted that the adoption of pop-up stores of mature brands operating in the Lebanese market depends on the brand's strategy and its expectations of the project. As for developing brands, pop-up stores are a means of gaining access to a market, building an address book or improving visibility while hoping to sell the collections offered. Boustani (2020) highlights different reasons for adopting pop-up stores.

In Middle Eastern contexts, ephemeral stores are tools for testing the market, for experimenting and for exploring a distribution channel. It is through these stores that brands can present concepts "without being judged" and without compromising their identity. Depending on the brand's distribution strategy, a pop-up store can be a way to help brands sell or liquidate their products. They also present an opportunity to unveil exclusive or limited collections. Ephemeral stores are communicated through social networks and their brief appearance is in itself a means of communication. They are social events, a "happening" that puts the brand in direct contact with consumers. What mainly benefits the brand from this exchange is the direct feedback it can collect and analyse.

Researchers have also studied the acceptability of pop-up stores as an innovative business strategy and as a tool to improve consumer shopping experience (Niehm et al., 2007); they highlighted consumer socio-demographic profiles. For instance, young consumers are more informed about pop-up stores and reported having had an experience with the format. Demand and interest in visiting a pop-up store may increase among older consumers as well as they have become more active, more socially engaged and more tech savvy. Previous research demonstrated that age has a significant effect on consumer's awareness experience in ephemeral stores. These young consumers reported that malls and department stores were places where they mostly found ephemeral stores.

Academic research was also interested in understanding pop-up stores and identifying or categorizing them. Pomodoro (2013) emphasized on four types that reflect the polyvalent nature of ephemeral stores (Figure 0.1).

A "concept store": The ephemeral store increases awareness and develops brand image. The store visit is then designed to generate a holistic and memorable brand experience, which puts the consumer in close connection with the brand. This category borrows the "flagship stores" formula except that in the case of ephemeral stores it is the brand experience that is reinforced by the temporary nature of the store. The brand wants consumers to be intensely involved and able to produce a personalized experience during their visit. "Concept stores" spaces are spectacular, thematic and multi-sensory; all retail design elements are designed to communicate a coherent visual identity. Events are built around the brand concept and are intended to create a multi-sensory and interactive brand experience. Consumers who visit the ephemeral store are invited to live an exciting, emotional and memorable experience.

A "community store": The ephemeral store is designed to support the brand/consumer emotional relationship to increase the feeling of belonging to the brand's community. In this case, the social event or "happening" becomes the key strategy. The ephemeral store's atmosphere remains a crucial element where these events take place and where everything is designed to increase the opportunities for exchange between the brand and consumers.

A "test store": A pop-up store can be a way to pre-test a new brand concept or a new range of products. The brand can experiment with a new market or even get started on a low budget through the "test store". Consequently, the store is designed as a market research tool: It is considered as a real "observatory" of the behaviours, attitudes and purchasing motivations of visitors.

A "sustainable temporary" store: Ephemeral stores are also used more and more in the eco-sustainable trend. Like other traditional retail formats, they seem to fit into the growing focus on sustainable and green lifestyles. An ephemeral store should then be conceived as an evolution of more traditional formats, although enriched with other promotional instruments, a longer shelf life and greater media exposure.

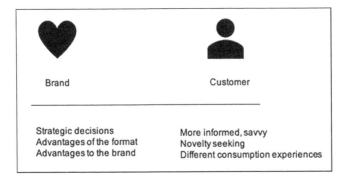

Figure 0.1 Retail formats that interest brands and customers.

Studies based on the concept of consumer experience or the co-creation of value drew on the DART (Dialogue, Access, Risk assessment, Transparency) model (Prahalad & Ramaswamy, 2004) that analysed the potential for value co-creation. It has been high-lighted that exceptional dialogues take place in ephemeral store contexts (Russo Spena et al., 2012). To foster an engaged dialogue, they offer their consumers access to knowledge, tools and expertise that allow the latter to experience products and services in an un-precedented way. The layout of the ephemeral store space promotes access to information and knowledge through the presence of tech-nological, virtual or media supports. It also includes a socializa-tion area separate from the point-of-sale area; it is in this area that the consumer will be able to enjoy a multi-sensory experience. The pop-up store's atmospheric design evokes brand values more ap-pealingly by tapping into the activation of consumers' five senses. Finally, location plays a very important role in promoting access to the experience. Indeed, it ensures high visibility of the temporary event. Customers have the opportunity to better assess the advan-tages and disadvantages associated with their decisions in the value creation process following their visit to a pop-up store. The possi-bility of interacting with the brand (through the technological tools offered and its representatives) and of testing or living the unique experience offered reassures consumers and encourages them to make purchases or make decisions. Finally, in terms of transpar-ency, pop-up stores have an important communicative purpose. Brands encourage the temporary experience to share information, values and emotions with consumers.

Ephemeral stores can greatly contribute to the amplification of relationships with customers. In the context of temporary store activations (Lowe et al., 2018), brands can have the opportunity to reach out to new customers and increase their level of awareness in the market, as well as increase their level of engagement with current customers. Temporary retail activations are also seen as brand–consumer exchange opportunities. The link between positive emotions and consumer engagement is induced by all experiences that the brand offers. Multi-sensory temporary retail spaces are an effective way to engage consumers through brand experiences. Serendipity is defined as a happy event and is a factor that largely contributes to the success of temporary retail activations. Despite the resources invested in planning temporary retail activations, brands recognize that the consumer experience is also created by independent and uncontrollable elements. Ephemeral stores are only successful when they are a true reflection of the brand's identity, when they mirror their environment and when they speak the consumer's language or appeal to the consumer's expectations.

An ephemeral store's atmosphere has a major role in attracting consumers, offering them opportunities of interacting with the brand and affecting their emotions or behaviour (Boustani, 2019). Researchers studied the pop-up store's atmosphere and how it might affect customer emotions and behaviours (Boustani & Lemoine, 2019). In a traditional store context, atmospheric stimuli could be manipulated to affect consumer reactions. Contrary to the results presented in academic literature on traditional stores, the atmospheric dimension of (Lebanese) pop-up stores have a limited impact on the emotional reactions of customers. The atmospheric "social" dimension positively affects emotional reactions of consumers who visit ephemeral points of sale. This aspect dominates any other form of stimulation at any given time and encourages people to spend more time, turns their visit into a hedonic escape, and serves as a window for pleasant socializing, reuniting or exploring. A pop-up store's audience acts as a magnet attracting people looking for a fun aspect, to spend time, to have fun, to socialize, to mingle with people and to be a part of the event (Boustani, 2019).

The aesthetic atmospheric dimension of Middle Eastern ephemeral stores does not influence consumer intentions, which contradicts previous research. Lebanese consumers feel that they must "experience" the event otherwise they will fear "being left out" and will not be at the "right time with the right crowd". Research results have shown that Lebanese consumers may react differently to pop-up stores than European or North American consumers. This may be due to the recent nature of the phenomenon in a local context, or it may be due to the strong social influences which crush any shopping opportunities during the event and instead centralize towards socialization and exchange.

Luxury brands have been adopting pop-up stores to meet different objectives and benefit from the many advantages of these store formats. To list a few, pop-up stores allow luxury brands to touch different audiences in different markets or touch a younger audience. They also help in testing new concepts, presenting product lines and so on. A luxury brand pop-up store's experience has been proven to be influenced by the word of mouth. A previous study has shown that pop-up stores are an effective experiential marketing tool (Klein et al., 2016) as they amplify a brand's experience and stimulate positive word of mouth. Moreover, it was highlighted that the hedonic purchase value of pop-up stores, the uniqueness of the store and its atmosphere positively affect word of mouth intentions towards a luxury brand. In the case of luxury brands, brand experience plays an important role in mediating the effects of hedonic shopping value and pop-up store atmosphere on WOM word of mouth. The brand experience acts as an important mediating variable between consumers' perception of store characteristics and their intentions to spread the word of mouth (WOM). The challenge of positioning luxury brands in the face of new consumer groups is being resolved through the adoption of pop-up stores. These stores are effective experiential marketing tools that increase exposure to the brand and induce positive word of mouth sharing among these new consumers. Most of the academic research adopting the subject of pop-up stores has focused on studying consumer intentions (or behavioural intentions) and attitudes towards these types of stores, understanding the acceptability and adoption by customer types, or attempting to categorize pop-up stores and providing an adequate typology.

Focusing on the ephemeral store, this book aims to provide a clear understanding of what it is, how it developed and why it gained importance in today's busy retail scene. As many brands are adopting ephemeral stores into their distribution channels or using them as unique touchpoints, this book proposes a categorization of "ephemeral retail" that explains different ephemeral store vocations based on different brand strategies and objectives.

Chapter 1 looks at ephemeral stores that have been appearing for the past decade. An "exposé" aims at presenting different cases of different brand categories (for instance fast fashion, luxury fashion, food, music) and sorting them by year. This chapter will highlight the array of brands adopting ephemeral stores, how they have done this, how they have communicated this, how much time they made these stores last and so on. After having drawn this timeline, the chapter synthesizes the gathered information about ephemeral retail and shows how these retail formats have grown and have matured.

As there is no exact definition of ephemeral retail to date and the concept is constantly evolving, it is important to attempt presenting different explanations on ephemeral stores or pop-up stores. Throughout Chapter 2, readers will be able to understand what is an ephemeral store, its unique features and its characteristics. The chapter does not pretend to provide an absolute definition of the term, but it will advance enough explanations from which the reader can draw a clear understanding of what ephemeral stores are.

Ephemeral retailing is straddling between distribution and communications; in fact, the few studies that have been interested in the subject have shown that these stores can be marketing tools, distribution channels, foreign operation modes, a temporary reflection of flagship stores or concept stores. Chapter 3 looks at these studies and aims at answering whether ephemeral stores are isolated communication or distribution channels, or whether ephemeral stores are considered amongst a brand's omnichannel perspective.

Is retail's evolution closing the loop with ephemeral stores? Is retail being redirected towards one-on-one and simplistic formats? After having explained the evolution of retail and having attempted to define and categorize it, Chapter 4 looks at how ephemeral stores found their natural place in an ever-changing retail environment.

References

Alexander, B., Nobbs, K. & Varley, R., 2018. The growing permanence of pop-up outlets within the international location strategies of fashion retailers. *International Journal of Retail & Distribution Management*, 46(5), pp. 487–506.

Boustani, G., 2019. *Ephemeral retailing: Pop-up stores in a postmodern consumption era.* Routledge, p. 116.

Boustani, G., 2020. *Ephemeral store adoption by brands.* Paris: International Marketing Trends Conference.

Boustani, G. & Lemoine, J-F., 2019. The influence of a retail store's atmosphere on consumer's reactions: The case of ephemeral stores, 6th French-Austrian-German Workshop on Consumer Behaviour. November 21–22, 2019, Nancy, France.

Chen, W.-C. & Fiore, A. M., 2017. Factors affecting Taiwanese consumers' responses toward pop-up retail. *Asia Pacific Journal of Marketing and Logistics*, 29(2), pp. 370–392.

De Lassus, C., 2012. Les pop-up stores de luxe: entre lieu mythique et endroit éphémère, une analyse sémiotique. *Colloque Etienne Thil*, Lille, France, Oct.

Fowler, K. & Bridges, E., 2010. Consumer innovativeness: Impact on expectations, perceptions, and choice among retail formats. *Journal of Retailing and Consumer Services*, 17, pp. 492–500.

Jones, P., Comfort, D. & Hillier, D., 2017. A commentary on pop up shops in the UK. *Property Management*, 35(5), pp. 545–553.

Kim, H., Fiore, A., Niehm, L. & Jeong, M., 2010. Psychographic characteristics affecting behavioral intentions towards pop-up retail. *International Journal of Retail & Distribution Management*, 38(2), pp. 133–154.

Klein, J. F., Falk, T., Esch, F.-R. & Gloukhovtsev, A., 2016. Linking pop-up brand stores to brand experience and word of mouth: The case of luxury retail. *Journal of Business Research*, 69(12), pp. 5761–5767.

Lowe, J., Maggioni, I. & Sands, S., 2018. Critical success factors of temporary retail activations: A multi-actor perspective. *Journal of Retailing and Consumer Services*, 40, pp. 175–185.

Niehm, L. S., Ann Marie, F., Jeong, M. & Kim, H.-J., 2007. Pop-up retail's acceptability as an innovative business strategy and enhancer of the consumer shopping experience. *Journal of Shopping Center Research*, 13(7), pp. 1–30.

Picot-Coupey, K., 2012. Pop-up stores and the international development of retail networks. *International marketing trends conference*, Venice, Italy, Jan.

Picot-Coupey, K., 2014. The pop-up store as a foreign operation mode (FOM) for retailers. *International Journal of Retail & Distribution Management*, 42(7), pp. 643–670.

Pomodoro, S., 2013. Temporary retail in fashion system: An explorative study. *Journal of Fashion Marketing and Management: An international Journal*, 17(3), pp. 341–352.

Prahalad, C. & Ramaswamy, V., 2004. Co-creation experiences: The next practice in value creation. *Journal of Interactive Marketing*, 3, pp. 5–14.

Russo Spena, T., Caridà, A., Colurcio, M. & Melia, M., 2012. Store experience and co-creation: The case of temporary shop. *International Journal of Retail & Distribution Management*, 40(1), pp. 21–40.

Taube, J. & Warnaby, G., 2017. How brand interaction in pop-up shops influences consumers' perceptions of luxury fashion retailers. *Journal of Fashion Marketing and Management: An International Journal*, 21(3), pp. 385–399.

1 From retail to ephemeral retail

1.1 Bringing traditional stores closer to ephemeral stores

1.1.1 An evolution from traditional marketing to experiential marketing

It has been argued that marketing research is most valued when it is placed in a framework that goes beyond a specific event, and therefore that will study the role of marketing in a broader economic and social context (Savitt, 1980). Although marketing research was established in 1936, it was not until the 1980s that the field of marketing became institutionalized with regular conferences, formal associations, newsletters and websites (Witkiwski & Jones, 2016). Marketing has become a real discipline in its own right, with reasonably distinct methods of generating and presenting knowledge heavily influenced by training and academic expectations. It has evolved from a product orientation to an experiential orientation which encompasses customer-centred practices. At a retail level, customer access to brand offerings has also evolved and the conception of retail spaces and retail practices has also followed the experiential orientation.

Focused on spending (Hirschman & Holbrook, 1982) and supply, traditional marketing approaches have evolved through a logic of focusing on the consumer and then moving towards a consumer/distributor relationship. At the very opposite of the spectrum, the development of experiential marketing is a result of the existential desire of the current consumer who seeks to consume out of desire rather than necessity. For experiential marketing, the consumer buys more for the emotional experience he can get and less for the offer's functional attributes (Badot & Cova, 2003); experiential marketing therefore leads to more impulsive than thoughtful purchases (Andrieu et al., 2004).

An experiential marketing approach would highly invest in the retail environment as well as other online/offline brand touchpoints. When in contact with the environment, the consumer is immersed in an experience, but this experience is understood as both a "process" and a "final state to be reached" (Carù & Cova, 2006). Marketing has evolved towards meeting customer expectations and has become more controlled by them (Table 1.1).

Ephemeral stores or pop-up stores found their way into brand strategic plans and customer's hearts. At the times when customers looked for more experiences and for consumption practices that made more sense to them, ephemeral stores were a perfect blend of hints of communications and sales presented in an experiential format.

1.2 Descriptive statistics of pop-up stores around the world

Following the 2008 recession, individual private spending was seriously affected and reduced (KPMG, 2009; Burgess, 2012; Smajovic & Warfvinge, 2014). About 7,000 physical stores were closed as operational costs grew and revenues remained flat (PWC, 2017). That year also saw an increase of 5.1% in store vacancy rates, which grew and reached 14.5% in 2014. Other statistics showed an increase of 12.3% in store vacancy for traditional physical stores and 13.2% for stores in shopping centres. Due to a lack of funding, lack of completion of the targeted turnover or lack of means of spending in terms of promotions and communication (Trendwatching, 2004), the majority of brands have turned to pop-up stores for their business. So, the recession was a trigger for pop-up stores (Boxall, 2012; CradlePoint, 2012; Tomlinson, 2014). The main recognized handicap of traditional physical commerce was above all linked to timid consumer spending. As a result, specialized retailers grew and positioned themselves more clearly in the market. Trade has become more polarized and fragmented in 2020, and has presented itself in an increasingly demarcated fashion.

The pop-up industry has grown to around $10 billion in sales according to "PopUp Republic". Indeed, since the launch of this organization in 2012, more than 30,000 stores, restaurants and pop-up spaces have used the site to promote their pop-ups (Popup Republic, n.d.). A recent article published online in *Business Insider* demonstrated a positive relationship between the opening of pop-up stores and online sales. The more the brand invested in

Table 1.1 From traditional to experiential marketing

Traditional marketing	Relationship and marketing	Experiential marketing
The beginning of the marketing concept in 1910 when we sought to understand the agricultural markets and the role of all actors (institutions, distributors, users, consumers) in price formation. The concept is structured around a vision of social and economic processes related to the market: a "marketing system" (Pras, 2012).	New customers, described as existential, have become less responsive to traditional marketing stimuli. This has prompted brands to add new elements to the marketing mix which are "personnel, format and presentation" (Constantinides, 2006). Brands have therefore taken action on the sales environment to offer customers "hedonic rewards" that enhance their shopping activities (Lemoine, 2005). With the advent of relationship marketing, the goal was to find products or services for customers and not the other way around (Badot & Cova, 2003). In addition to the traditional "4 Ps", brands focus on selecting suppliers and their service delivery and designing their physical environments to meet the needs of target customers (Fowler & Bridges, 2010).	The strategic approach to experiential marketing assumes that brands develop a "set of attributes loaded with meaning and values" in order to provide a distinctive experience when the customer visits the brand (Ochs & Remy, 2006), which offers a surprising or even "spectacular and extravagant" environment (Carù & Cova, 2006). Other research points out that experiential marketing goes beyond consumer-brand contact at the point of sale as it integrates all points of contact of retailers with consumers (Niehm et al., 2007) and amplifies the essence of the brand.

Traditional marketing developed in response to the industrial age (Schmitt, 1999). Then appeared the concept of marketing mix. First approached by Borden in 1942, then approached by Culliton who, in 1948, described the decision-maker as a "mixer of ingredients", the marketing mix was used to express the fact that management could achieve certain predetermined objectives by the manipulation of variables that McCarthy, later, defined by the "4 Ps". Likewise, the concept of marketing management also appeared in the 1950s, defined as decision-making concerning products, promotion and distribution channels (Flambard-Ruaud, 1997). The marketing concept is particularly resilient. While it has evolved and deformed according to the times and the environment, it returned to its initial form in the 1990s, admittedly transformed but staying in phase with its fundamentals (Pras, 2012).

The first attempts to enrich the point-of-sale experience began with sensory marketing (Antéblian et al., 2013). It is a source of production of emotional effects (Bonnin, 2002), and is therefore a set of controlled action variables that the brand controls to create a specific multi-sensory atmosphere around its offer (Filser, 2003). Moreover, brands have begun to pay more attention to customer senses previously neglected at the point of sale: hearing, smell, taste and touch (Daucé & Rieunier, 2002) (Spence et al., 2014). When designing atmospheric stores (Lemoine, 2004), distributors naturally use atmospheric variables to elicit emotional responses from customers. These emotions provide joy, excitement and a satisfied customer mood (Srinivasan & Srivastava, 2010).

Experiential marketing from a brand perspective:

Three phenomena have taken place simultaneously in the business environment and have caused companies and brands to abandon traditional marketing to create experiences for their customers. These three phenomena, namely the ubiquity of information technology, brand supremacy and the ubiquity of communications and entertainment, were the first signs of an entirely new marketing approach; the experience economy (Schmitt, 1999). Later on, the emergence of the experience economy and experiential marketing gave birth to an experiential approach to retail (Shilpha & Rajnish, 2013).

(*Continued*)

Traditional marketing	*Relationship and marketing*	*Experiential marketing*
Traditional marketing has become less effective nowadays (Niehm et al., 2007) and consumers are less reactive to its transactional strategies. Traditional marketing concepts and methodologies describe the nature of products, consumer behaviour and competitive activity in the market. They are used to develop new products; plan product lines and brand extensions; design communications; and respond to competitive activities (Rhee & Mehra, 2006).	Brands have also considered the interplay between variables because consumers assess a shopping environment in a holistic way: appropriate background music, bright lighting, or scents to stimulate and awaken or, conversely, to soothe them (Antéblian et al., 2013).	To avoid the risk of trivializing consumption experiences by considering the consumer as a passive spectator, the goal of experiential marketing should translate the essence or associations of the brand "into a set of tangibles, physical, interactive experiences" (Chen & Fiore, 2017) and "entertaining" (Russo Spena et al., 2012). This approach places a strong emphasis on the customer experience and views consumption as a holistic experience (Frazer & Stiehler, 2014).
Traditional marketing has been characterized by a narrow definition of the offer, the definition of competition and the benefits of the brand's offer. Management methods were analytical, quantitative and verbal (Schmitt, 1999). As a key element of the marketing mix, the assortment represented a strategic positioning tool for customer acquisition and retention. Decisions regarding quality, price levels and variety of the assortment determined a retailer's position in the market (Hansen & Singh, 2009) (Bauer et al., 2012).	Research has provided evidence of important point-of-sale atmosphere interactive effects on consumers' perception of brand image and has found that perception is inherently multi-sensory (Spence et al., 2014). Researchers also found that consumers who perceive retail environments as more pleasant display a higher level of satisfaction and a positive experience towards the brand. (Daucé & Rieunier, 2002).	Experiential marketing suggests a holistic manipulation of "experiential" elements that will lead to multi-sensory experiences (Foster & McLelland, 2014). For brands, one of the purposes of experiential marketing is to design experiential contexts that differentiate them (Antéblian et al., 2013) and that lead them to obtain competitive advantages through the entertainment offered. However, these contexts must be integrated at every point of touch with the brand: in the store, through marketing communication and advertising, through the website and at events or other brand activities (Niehm et al., 2007).

As for consumers in the traditional marketing era, they were seen as rational decision-makers (Schmitt, 1999). For most of the 20th century, customers were "product takers" and "price takers", accepting goods dedicated from suppliers (Slywotzky et al., 2000).

The development of the marketing mix consisted of "conveying the right message on the right product, at the right price, in the right place, at the right time and to the right person". With the "passive 4 Ps" application, retailers and other intermediaries were seen as secondary actors in the marketing process. Their responsibilities were confined to the functions of product storage and resale.

Experiential Marketing from a Consumer Perspective:

Consumers were seen as "rational decision-makers" before the new experiential approach offered a different view of consumer behaviour; they are now considered to be "thinkers and doers" and as someone whose role goes beyond the act of purchasing (Gentile et al., 2007). Contemporary consumers are therefore in search of meanings or in search of the meaning provided by products (Camus & Poulain, 2008). In addition, the act of buying will be replaced by an immersion in the consumption experience (Russo Spena et al., 2012). Consumers, "rational and emotional" (Frazer & Stiehler, 2014), seek satisfying shopping and consumption experiences that are (Bustamante & Rubio, 2017) emotionally charged (Camus & Poulain, 2008).

(Continued)

Traditional marketing	*Relationship and marketing*	*Experiential marketing*
Unfortunately, traditional marketing concepts offer little guidance for taking advantage of the emerging experiential economy (Schmitt, 1999). Over the past two decades, as customers have become more sophisticated and have gained more power over the buying process, they have ceased to be price takers. However, they are still product takers. Even as suppliers have tailored their offerings to increasingly thinner segments of the customer base, buyers are ultimately forced to settle for the best approximation of what they want. But with the system of choice, customers are no longer product takers; they are product manufacturers (Slywotzky et al., 2000). In these current times, the marketing mix is still there, except that it is managed from the consumer's point of view and its aim is to deliver a unique experience to consumers. Marketing is no longer satisfied with the "4 Ps" mix; it has evolved over the past few years from relational, experiential and value perspectives (Sénécal, 2015).		Following inclinations towards engaging relationships (Niehm et al., 2007), experiential marketing offers a response to the existential desire of consumers (Russo Spena et al., 2012) who are in the search for "sensitive" experiences (Camus & Poulain, 2008) that they will be able to express during their visits to the commercial sphere. It has also been shown that the production of experiences is not restricted to the point of sale; they occur when consumers look for products or services, when they buy them and when they consume them (Barkus et al., 2009). Experiential marketing therefore creates memorable experiences, necessarily involving consumer participation and goes beyond needs (Srinivasan & Srivastava, 2010). To be meaningful, the experience must be co-created between the brand and its customers (Russo Spena et al., 2012).

ephemeral locations, the more online sales grew, proving that the marriage between virtual stores and pop-up stores leads to success (Addady, 2016).

Despite their popularity, pop-up store adoption remained mainly limited to the United States and the United Kingdom until the year 2011. Other countries later followed the adoption of this type of retailing (Haas & Schmidt, 2016). A report published in 2014 indicates that a 16% increase in these outlets took place between 2003 and 2009 in the United States, and this especially in the following cities, which accommodate the most pop-up stores: Los Angeles, New York, London, Paris, Berlin, Stockholm, Tokyo and Shanghai (Nicasio, 2015).

There is a significant presence of digital technologies in physical ephemeral stores. A third of sales made in physical stores in 2015 was influenced by these technologies; this rate attenuated by 50% in 2015 (Deloitte, 2014). French consumers, for example, are adopting technological tools and are becoming more and more connected. 50.7% of the French population in 2017 was connected to the internet via a smartphone (Comarch, 2018) and spent a considerable amount of time on digital platforms as well as social networks. 58% of opinions shared online influence the attitudes and expectations of consumers (Influencia, 2017). It is through the design of the pop-up store, its location and its interiors that the relationship between the brand and the consumer is established. Designed theatrically, they are considered an art form (Picot-Coupey, 2014) and appeal to hedonic consumers, thanks to their novelties and their distinctive characters in terms of the point of sale's atmosphere, the selection merchandise, communications… From an empirical point of view, there is ample evidence to support the new conceptualization of the store as an environment of experience, allowing sensory, emotional and social connections (Kim et al., 2010; Russo Spena et al., 2012).

1.2.1 A decennial census of pop-up stores

Given the increase of pop-up store brand adoption in recent years, it seemed important to census different brands that have manifested through pop-ups. The objective of creating a timeline is to trace, over the last decade, the increase in the adoption of pop-up stores by brands, and to show the diversity of brands and their activities. Finally, the objective of this census is to show that this trend is firmly establishing itself as a means of communication and distribution and is gaining an important place among consumers.

According to the inventory of the different cases of brands adopting pop-up stores and the knowledge retained following their chronological presentation, it is noted that pop-up store brand adoption undergoes a continuous growth rate for various industries such as fashion, cosmetics, drugstore, cars, food, technology or sport. The list is becoming more and more varied and shows that pop-up store adoption is not reserved to a defined industry. Moreover, it can be noticed that the adoption of pop-up stores has kept increasing during the past decade.

Below is a census of pop-up stores during the last decade in France (for consistency purposes, the decennial observation looked at one market only): Table 1.2 shows some brands which have adopted ephemeral stores between the period 2008 and 2020.[1]

This census reveals important aspects related to the adoption of pop-up stores by brands. This retail format is agile, is flexible and helps different brands meet infinite possibilities.

A pop-up store can last anywhere from a day to a few months. A 30-day period seems like the average lifespan of a pop-up store. It is however noticed that the shorter the duration of the store (ranging from a day to a week), the more likely it is going to tend towards event-based or promotional stores; on the other hand, the longer the duration of the ephemeral store (on average one month or more), the more we go towards setting up an ephemeral store with a commercial aspect.

The pop-up store's location is meticulously thought out and chosen to target customers and benefit from dwellers who may happen to be in the area. Our chronological data collection makes France, Paris, our research core. However, we notice the different choices adopted by different brands to locate their pop-up stores: in the Parisian centre, in districts far from the centre, in train stations, in chic districts, in young districts, in shopping centres, gardens, hotels or on the street. The choice of location is relative to the brand's identity, its target customers and the objective it is interested in achieving through the establishment of the pop-up store.

An equally decisive factor in the success or failure of a pop-up store is its "timing" or the time during which it will be revealed. Brands choose a particular event, party or season relevant to the brand and to the pop-up store's purpose to capture the desired outcome. Brands may choose to appear among many dates such as the Christmas and holidays season, music festivals, Fashion Weeks and back-to-school periods. They could also have their calendars based on which they can create and communicate events. In many

Table 1.2 Summary census of pop-up stores over the last decade in France

Year	Brand/activity	Pop-up store's duration and location	Pop-up store format and type	Pop-up store's objective
2008	Nike/sport	60 days/Paris	Virtual/commercial	Olympic games
2009	Uniqlo/fashion	90 days/Paris, le Marais	Boutique/commercial	Presentation of emblematic products
	Hema/home	150 days/Paris, Train station	Train station/commercial	Building brand awareness
2010	Tripiers/products	4 days/Paris, rue du Vertbois	Revolving counter/ commercial	Product presentation
	Office Hollandais/flowers	3 days/Paris, St. Germain, Bercy Train station, Montparnasse Train station	Vegetation Bubbles/ commercial	Promotion of indoor plants
	Kronenbourg/beer	15 days/Paris, rue de Rivoli	Boutique/commercial	Help people discover the main stages of beer making
	Mixology/alcohol	30 days/Paris, Montparnasse Train station	Bar/commercial	Tasting of cocktails inspired by molecular cuisine
2011	Côte d'Or/chocolate	30 days/Paris, rue St. Honoré	Boutique/commercial	Provide consumers with a sensory experience
	Uniqlo/fashion	30 days/Paris, la Défense	Train station/commercial	Announce the expansion of the store
	Uniqlo/fashion	30 days/Paris, Charles de Gaulle	Train station/commercial	The brand launches a first-of-its-kind pop-up
	Krug/champagne	10 days/Paris	Roof of a building under construction/ non-commercial	Brand of champagne accompanying a chef's menus
2012	Karl by Karl Lagerfeld/ fashion	1day/Paris, place St. Germain (x)days/Online	Applications iPad connected/commercial ePop-up/commercial	Exceptional launch of the brand
	Fendi/fashion	6 days/Paris	Boutique/commercial	Sale of limited editions of the brand's flagship product
	Casa Barilla/culinary	9 days/Paris	Boutique/commercial	Celebrate the art of cooking
	Danette/culinary			

(*Continued*)

Year	Brand/activity	Pop-up store's duration and location	Pop-up store format and type	Pop-up store's objective
2013	PlayStation/game	(x)days/Paris	Connected space/non-commercial	Pre-release product testing
	Aruba tourism/travel agency	1 day/Paris	Connected space/non-commercial	Make a greeting card
	So, cream/culinary	30 days/Paris, Val d'Europe	Centre commercial/non-commercial	Let consumers freely compose their desserts
	Technology	30 days/Paris	Centre commercial/commercial	The product output
	Bic/product	10 days/rue de Roi de Sicile	Hotel/non-commercial	Celebrate the brand's holiday
	Felurence/florist	26 days/Paris, Boulogne	Boutique/non-commercial	Invite in a friendly way the universe of the brand
	TicTac/culinary	15 days/Paris, Montmartre	City Hall/commercial	Invitation of internet users to customize, then organization of an event in collaboration with artists
	Happy Socks/fashion	30 days/Paris	Space/non-commercial	Christmas event in collaboration with an artist
	Ferrero Rocher/chocolate	15 days/Paris, St. Lazare	Boutique/commercial	Delight visitors and put them in the Christmas mood
	Converse	30 days/Paris	Giant fir/commercial	Offer a "tune & repair" service
	Canal +	120 days/Paris	Boutique/commercial, Centre commercial/commercial	Interactive and fun store to test new services
2014	Moleskine/stationary	(x) days/Paris, St. Honoré	Boutique/commercial	Test the brand's potential in France
	Screeneo/technology	10 days/Paris, St. Lazare	Train station/non-commercial	Presentation of the brand's products
	Kenzo/fashion	30 days/Paris	Commercial centre/commercial	Unveil the capsule collection
	Jeep/cars	(x) days/Paris, Val d'Europe	Commercial centre/commercial	Allow customers to assess the capacity of their 4 × 4
	Toyota/cars	2 days/Paris, rue Muller	Commercial centre/non-commercial	Collaborations with artists, animations and culinary events
	MAC/cosmetics	30 days/Paris, Val d'Europe	Street/non-commercial	Unique and interactive make-up experience through touchpads
	YvesRocher/cosmetics	90 days/Paris	Commercial centre/commercial	Beauty makeovers done by professionals
	So Glad/cosmetics	30 days/Paris, Val d'Europe	Commercial centre/commercial	Treat consumers with well-deserved manicure breaks
	Habana club/alcool	75 days/Paris	Coffee shop/commercial	The brand has given the café the appearance of a Cuban alleyway
	Obey your body/cosmetics	120 days/Paris, Créteil	Commercial centre/commercial	Marketing the brand's products online

2015			
La Redoute/fashion	90 days/Paris	Container/commercial	Customers can touch, try or discover by ordering through electronic terminals
Mon Look/fashion	30 days/Paris	Event/commercial	Offers the public a shopping and sharing experience of African culture
Natura Brasil/cosmetics	30 days/Paris, Belle épine, Créteil, Ecully	Commercial centre/commercial	The brand goes out to meet its customers to promote and test its products
Yves Rocher/cosmetics	90 days/Paris	Boutique/commercial	Install a pop-up while the store is under construction
H&M/fashion	1 day/Paris, porte de Versailles	Concert/non-commercial	A fashion brand offering free music concerts
Etsy/fashion	3 days/Paris, Rue du Vertbois	Boutique/commercial	Creators who want to launch their brands
Videdressing/fashion	90 days/Paris et grandes villes	Fashion truck/commercial	The community site goes from virtual to real
Marionnaud/cosmetics	90 days/Paris	Beauty truck/commercial	Mobile boudoir offering free make-up sessions
Les choses jolies/start-up brands	30 days/Bayonne	Exhibition/commercial	Reviving the city centre
Hermès/fashion	20 days/Paris, Berges de la Seine	Exhibition/ non-commercial	Development of the area with dreamlike and interactive paintings, highlighting the brand's know-how
Timberland/fashion	30 days/Paris Caumartin	Boutique/commercial	Celebrate a new collection with the possibility of customization
Zagatub/kids	16 days/Paris, Créteil	Boutique/commercial	Objects and stories for children, discoveries, ideas for Christmas
Vente Unique/furniture	30 days/Paris, Créteil	Centre commercial/ commercial	Items at reduced prices and which can be ordered on site
Tati/fashion	45 days/Paris, St. Lazare	Train station/commercial	Products in collaboration with Chantal Thomas. 500,000 flowers spread over 2,000 m^2. The flowers will be offered to the town hall to be installed in various places in the city
Yoplait/culinary	4 days/Paris, Tours Eiffel	Garden/commercial	Promoting the values of the brand.

(Continued)

Year	Brand/activity	Pop-up store's duration and location	Pop-up store format and type	Pop-up store's objective
2016	Muji/fashion	7 days/Paris	Exhibition/non-commercial	Exhibition retracing the evolution of the brand's visual communication
	Giorgio Armani/cosmetics	60 days/Paris, le Marais	Armani box/commercial	Make-up in an attractive decoration
	Ghd/hair care	28 days/Paris, rue St. Jacques	Boutique/commercial	Explain to visitors how to master curlers and other straighteners
	Dove/cosmetics	90 days/Paris	Boutique/commercial	Meet the experts, participate in workshops and personalize the brand's products
	La Manche/tourism	10 days/Paris	Commercial centre/non-commercial	Themed evening, presentation of products
2017	Previly et Netstore/start-up	20 days/Paris, rue Etienne Marcel	Boutique/commercial	Internet users vote for their favourite designer
	French Fashion/fashion	2 days/Paris, République	Hotel/commercial	Discover French designer collections
	Eden Being/fashion	30 days/Paris, rue du Faubourg St. Honoré	Hotel/commercial	A brand that brings together luxury products and that comes to settle in the hotel lobby
	Vestiaire Collective/fashion	101 days/Paris, St. Roch	Boutique/commercial	Collective cloakroom
	Carte d'Or/chocolate	90 days/Paris	Boutique/commercial	Ice creams, desserts, pastries

The list of brands engaging in pop-up stores continues to grow. We add to this list a few brands that have presented interesting projects since 2018 and till date.

Year	Brand/activity	Pop-up store's duration and location	Pop-up store format and type	Pop-up store's objective
2018-till date	L'univers du Studio Ghibli/gadgets	7 weeks/Paris	Ephemeral castle/commercial	Collection dedicated to movie characters
	Harry Potter/gadgets	90 days/Paris,	Store instore/commercial	Collections dedicated to fanatics
	Smukle/accessories	8 days/Paris, St. Germain des Près	Concept store/commercial	Collection of accessories
	Tatoo/tattoo	12 days/Paris, rue de Turenne	Space/commercial	Tattoo, jewellery and clothing
	Hello Body/beauty care and cosmetics	15 days/Paris, rue de la Ferronnerie	Boutique/commercial	Body and face care
	The Mindful Shop/well-being	13 days/Paris, Batignolles	Boutique/commercial and event-based	Collections dedicated to well-being and workshops
	Boutique des musées/gadgets	60 days/Paris, rue de Rivoli	Boutique/commercial	Gadgets and private collections
	Bettina Vermillon/footwear	1 week/Paris, au bon Marché	Concession/commercial	Shoe collection
	HomeCore/fashion	30 days/Paris, Champs Elysées	Concession/commercial	Clothing collections
	Sacai/fashion and home	30 days/Paris	Boutique/commercial	Clothing collections and home fashion

cases, seasonal brands highly rely on pop-up stores to promote their offering.

Moreover, the choice of location goes hand in hand with the pop-up store's format. This is when brands choose to come forward by opting for a look that is congruent with the location, the event and the clientele. In a garden, for example, a brand presented its ephemeral greenhouse-shaped store. Another set up a kiosk on the terrace of a shopping centre. Another brand placed a digital cube on Boulevard St. Germain to benefit from important customer dwell.

A pop-up store's theme (sometimes referred to as "concept") respects the brand's identity while offering consumers a different scenography albeit consistent with the location, the brand and the chosen format; this scenography may change during the pop-up store's life or can simply be reproduced with pop-up stores appearing at different locations. Note that the brand tells a story through its ephemeral store; it carefully chooses elements that reflect its identity and it can reveal several elements in a pop-up store or, again, in a sequel of pop-up stores. This tendency of repeatedly popping-up in several locations links the brand's pop-up stores and creates a mental thread that keeps a concise link between all of the brand's activities.

It is also important to note that an ephemeral store can be commercial or non-commercial, it may be physical or virtual. The choice of the ephemeral store's format is therefore closely linked to the objective of its launch. Several objectives can be gathered to unfold the reason why a brand sets up a pop-up store, and these will categorize the distribution or communication spheres. This does not preclude having ephemeral stores offering both entertainment and the possibility of sale. For example, when launching a capsule collection, a brand can offer consumers the opportunity to personalize their products, by offering on-site events and sewing workshops, and ultimately entice them to buy the product.

Ephemeral stores are agile and can help brands meet many objectives. For instance, brands can benefit from setting up a pop-up store when they are doing work in their physical stores; this will avoid loss of potential sales during the duration of the works. Pop-up stores reinforce the brand's notoriety. They help in launching a collection and presenting emblematic brand products. Through pop-up stores, brands can test products, test a location or even unveil a new product or collection. Besides, they can introduce customers to brand process or brand-specific experiences. Pop-up stores are great tools for providing customers with a sensory experience as they help them discover new concepts or products. Customers participate in the events that the brand has organized in the pop-up store, they communicate with brand representatives, exchange with them and get to share their opinions about the brand and its offering.

By offering consumers a different, innovative and unique experience, brands offer well thought-out pop-up stores that are geared towards consistency with the lifestyles and requirements of target consumers. These points of contact merge the physical with the digital through the implementation of connected and digitized materials: screens, touch pads, digital control terminals or live broadcasts. In short, the physical and the digital merge and become inseparable. Brands should value all communications and conversations that takes place on digital platforms as they are becoming part of the brand-customer conversation bubble. As internet users are registered on social networks, they are subsequently exposed to forums, messages, announcements, or are "tagged" or "mentioned"; they get access to brand information, talk to the brand or talk about it. If interest is built, internet users will come to physically meet the brand in its ephemeral store. They will publish geo-localized comments or photos and share them on social networks on which they are registered. In other cases, a passenger, interested or intrigued by the ephemeral store, can also send information, photos or videos with other members of his social or socio-virtual group. The process becomes a never-ending online/offline, physical/digital, personal/general exchange.

1.2.2 Ephemeral store interlintra influential variables

Pop-up stores borrow atmospheric characteristics from traditional stores. Their success depends on different variables that coexist, such as, to list a few, product selection, theme, seasonality or shelf life. For instance, a pop-up that is programmed to appear during the third week of December will probably be focused on Christmas and end-of year festivities and will be proposing products or events that relate to the location in which it is appearing. When a pop-up store appears in a specific location and at a precise time, it will "give flavour" (Boustani, 2019) to the environment by making it more dynamic and fun or by rejuvenating it.

The brand has a statute delimiting the nature of its commercial activity. Each brand has a specific objective it wishes to achieve and expectations relating to its projects; in the context of setting up pop-up store projects, the expectations of brands having specified a particular objective is an evaluation of the results obtained from the project. In special cases, the brand may make collaborations, with others from the same or from different industries, to help build a unique pop-up store. Guided by its objectives, the brand is developing its "ephemeral store". Aware of the advantages and disadvantages linked to the project, the brand wishes to offer an event or commercial pop-up store, and to present it through a format in which the interior is arranged so that it offers a route experiential to the visitor/consumer/client. The pop-up store is placed in the right place, offers the right products and the right price range is presented during the right season and for the desired lifespan.

Several "external influences" encourage brands or prevent them from setting up ephemeral stores. A national or local event of interest to the brand may encourage it to set up a pop-up store, yet space providers may not have the goods or locations or prices corresponding to the brand, thus preventing it from continuing to carry out its projects. If an ephemeral store has been presented by the brand, it will mobilize communication tools to transmit information or interact with targeted consumers or its customers. Digital platforms are effective means that can be adopted by the brand to share news about the pop-up store. These "connector links" help the brand to make its projects known more easily. Interested and "intrigued" consumers will flock to the pop-up store especially when they are in the business of engaging with the brand, having experiences or building relationships with the brand or with other consumers (Figure 1.1).

Many variables appear in a pop-up store or an ephemeral store's context. They can influence the pop-up store or can be influenced by its sudden appearance.

— The pop-up store's location: It's not strange for a brand to "pop up" pop-up stores in multiple locations (Deprez, 2018); art galleries, docks, abandoned buildings or trendy neighbourhoods (Edwards, 2017). These are known as "unrestricted places" (Monteiro, 2014). The nature of pop-up stores also allows them to be set up in various and unexpected locations (Giaimo, 2017) (Hughes, 2007); yet, most of the time, they favour vacant places relevant or more accessible to the target audience. These places are congruent with the brand's identity and positioning. They appear at the right time and respond meticulously to the brand's objectives (Picot-Coupey, n.d.) (Sophelle, Focus Report, 2017),

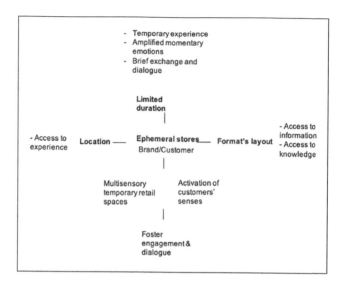

- Temporary experience
- Amplified momentary emotions
- Brief exchange and dialogue

Limited duration

- Access to experience

Location —— Ephemeral stores Brand/Customer —— Format's layout

- Access to information
- Access to knowledge

Multisensory temporary retail spaces

Activation of customers' senses

Foster engagement & dialogue

Figure 1.1 Brand/customer exchange in ephemeral store context.

such as testing an area (Schwab, 2014). Brands can also stand out through the choice of location when their intention is to transform a static place into a dynamic area (L'indépendant, 2017).

— The premises' layout: Pop-up stores are "magical" places that the brand creates (Yvernault, 2016) and that lie between physical and virtual spaces (Steimer, 2017). As the consumer is at the heart of this action, the atmosphere becomes friendly (Edwards, 2017) and lively (Liza, 2017). Brands have reinvented shops to make real places of entertainment (Comarch, 2018), experiential places (Rosenthal, 2009). Pop-up stores are equally well represented in physical and digital configurations (Deslandes, 2018) (Belloir, 2016).

— Technology: Technology is a driving force that fits into the logic of pop-up store designs; its use is an important tool (Giaimo, 2017) and has advantages for the brand and for the consumer. In an era of experiential and digital marketing, brand success will depend on the degree of connectivity with consumers (Cramer, Event Marketer, 2017). Technologies are materializing and transforming brand / customer relationships. Brands are undergoing a "digital divide", which means that the involvement of technology in brand strategy is no longer optional; it is a necessity (Deloitte, 2014). Once pop-up stores are operational, they need to collect, synthesize and analyse the collected data. This is how technology takes its place in the store's infrastructure (Sophelle, Focus Report, 2017). Equipped with automated and connected technology (Guingois, 2015), brands are more able to put forward a transition thread between digital and physical, which will make it possible to test and understand how consumers react (Swedberg, 2017) and will give them the power to shape their own experience (InsiderTrends, n.d.). As the information is available seven days a week and twenty-four hours a day, the consumer feels the power of control (KPMG, 2009) on the one hand and an engagement with the brand on the other hand (Deloitte, 2017). The "smartphone" becomes a tool for sharing and collecting data (Edwards, 2017) and facilitates the exchange and access to information, it has enabled brands to identify nearby consumers, to geo-locate them (BNP Paris Bas, 2014); it gave the client the possibility to share their photos, opinions, comments or feelings with the members of the peer group. To conclude, technology helps brands promote more flexible concepts (WeArePopup, 2017).

— The pop-up store's concept, theme or story: A pop-up store's interior is designed to stimulate consumer senses. This space is designed according to a theme (Martínez Navarro, 2016) or a story (Aubry & Souza, 2011) that is told through the decor and, of course, through the disseminated communications (Martínez Navarro, 2016). A "brand universe" is created (Yvernault, 2016) (Forbes, 2008) and organized according to the brand's needs and concerning its identity. The store type will indicate the presentation methods of collection, products or information on the site. As technological tools are inseparable from pop-up stores, they become an integral part of the store theme design and conception. This universe can be replicated with different repetitions or it can change with each appearance (Newton, 2017) as it can be specially designed for the occasion. Moreover, pop-up stores' atmospheric conception focuses on sensory stimulation. This emotional-based design approach tends towards the creation of customer experience (Martínez Navarro, 2016) and value creation.

— Collections or products: Consumers are now more interested in the brand, its identity, its history and its practices than in the products it offers. They demand to know more about the goods they buy, and how and by whom a product was made (Jones et al., 2017). In addition to location and design factors, researchers also say that the exclusivity and limited availability of products are crucial. Products offered in pop-up stores can generate effects such as purchasing incentives or incite customers to make instant purchases (Monteiro, 2014). Given the variety of objectives expected from pop-up stores, the different shapes and formats that they can take and the locations in which they materialize, the presentation of the collections or the products offered can also differ from what is expected of a "collection" in a traditional context. The presentation of products in this type of store must imperatively involve the customer's five senses (CPM experts, 2015). Then, depending on the brand's objectives, collections can be exclusive (Belloir, 2016) to the pop-up and its location, they can be personalized (Harel, 2016), capsule collections (Germack, 2014) or limited editions (Wang, 2018) (Schwab, 2014).

— The pop-up store's seasonality: Seasonality plays an important role in the implementation of pop-up stores (Wang, 2018) (Deprez, 2018) (Laparade, 2017). The seasonality of pop-up stores is not to be confused with seasonal stores (LaVito, 2017). Although the terms are closely associated, their meanings are not quite the same. Seasonality is very personal to the brand as it chooses the key moments during which customer contact and relationship with the store concept are in harmony and meet the brand's objectives and expectations. So, the brand capitalizes on the seasonal opportunities (Hékimian, 2018) that are relevant to it or indicates the moments that meet the specificities of the pop-up, thus creating its seasonality.

— The pop-up store's life cycle: Pop-up stores have a limited lifespan. They last on average 1 day and can live up to 18 months (Planchard, 2012) (Haas & Schmidt, 2016) (Deprez, 2018) (Harel, 2016).

— Landlords and space managers: Typically, landlords who lease commercial spaces or premises seek long-term, low-risk, regular-income leases with successful tenants. Pop-up stores are "good tenants" for landlords between long-term agreements, as they provide rent and physical activity at a location that was supposed to be vacant (Monteiro, 2014). Given the vacancy rates of premises and the difficulty of securing new conventional leases, landlords are becoming more flexible and more open to rent their spaces for short periods and therefore offer an alternative to the traditional lease (BFM TV., 2016).

— Third parties and service providers: Service or venue rental providers facilitate the work of brands wishing to launch into pop-up stores. These agents offer a search for the commercial space (Storefront, 2017) suited to the brand and meeting its objectives; digital platforms, such as Storefront or Appear Here, make it easier to book premises online (BFM TV., 2016) (WeArePopup, 2017); others simply relate the brand to the space (The Storefront, n.d.). Several agencies now offer event production services (Bouleau, 2017), scenographic production or retail operationalization (Barraud, 2017).

Note

1 To perform this census, a search was performed online, using the Google platform. The key words (pop-up store, pop-up shop, pop-up retail, ephemeral store) were used along with the corresponding year (from 2008 to 2020). Results that appeared on the top ten of the first page were selected and analysed.

References

Addady, M., 2016. Here's how many pop-up stores Amazon plans to open. [Online] Available at: http://fortune.com/2016/09/09/amazon-pop-up-stores/ [Accessed 17 01 2017].

Andrieu, F., Badot, O. & Mace, S., 2004. Hypermodernité et distribution: le cas du West Edmonton Mall. *Revue Management & Avenir*, Fevrier, (196), pp. 27–50.

Antéblian, B., Filser, M. & Roederer, C., 2013. L'expérience du consommateur dans le commerce de détail. Une revue de littérature. *Recherche et Applications en Marketing*, 28(3), pp. 84–114.

Aubry, F. & Souza, R., 2011. *The art and science of retail reinvention.* [Online] Available at: https://www.bcg.com/documents/file86012.pdf [Accessed 06 12 2017].

Badot, O. & Cova, B., 2003. Néo-marketing, 10 and après: pour une théorie critique de la consommation et du marketing réenchantés. *Revue Francaise du marketing*, Novembre, (195), pp. 79–94.

Barkus, J., Schmitt, B. & Zarantonelle, L., 2009. Brand experience: What is it? How is it measured? Does it affect loyalty? *Journal of Marketing*, 73(3), pp. 52–68.

Barraud, P., 2017. *Toulouse: un espace de « boutiques éphémères » va ouvrirses portes rue Alsace-Lorraine.* [Online] Available at: www. actu.fr [Accessed 06 12 2017].

Bauer, J. C., Kotouc, A. J. & Rudolph, T., 2012. What constitutes a « goodassortment »? A scale for measuring consumers' perceptions of an assortment offered in a grocery category. *Journal of Retailing and Consumer Services*, 19, pp. 11–26.

Belloir, M., 2016. *Dove lance un site ecommerce éphémère.* [Online] Available at: https://www.lsa-conso.fr/dove-lance-un-site-e-commerce-ephemere,248907 [Accessed 12 02 2018].

BFM TV., 2016. *Cette start-up française est devenue N°1 mondial du magasin éphémère.* [Online] Available at: http://bfmbusiness.bfmtv.com/entreprise/cette-start-up-francaise-est-devenue-n1-mondial-du-magasin-ephemere-1074744.html# [Accessed 12 02 2018].

BNP Paris Bas, 2014. *Social networks: Ephemeral proximitybased links the next big thing?* [Online] Available at: https://atelier.bnpparibas/en/smart-city/article/social-networks-ephemeral-proximity-based-links-big-thing [Accessed 24 11 2017].

Bonnin, G., 2002. Magasin et expérience de magasinage: le rôle de l'appropriation. *Décisions Marketing*, Octobre-Décembre, (28), pp. 65–75.

Bouleau, M.-S., 2017. *Le figaro.* [Online] Available at: http://www.lefigaro.fr/sortir-paris/2017/04/12/30004-20170412ARTFIG00048-my-pop-up-store-createur-de-magasins-ephemeres-sur-mesure.php [Accessed 13 11 2017].

Boustani, G., 2019. *Ephemeral retailing: Pop-up stores in a postmodern consumption era.* Routledge, p. 116.

Boxall, N., 2012. Are pop-up shops the answer to empty high streets? [Online] Available at: https://www.theguardian.com/money/2012/jul/20/pop-up-shops-empty-high-street [Accessed 12 02 2016].

Burgess, B., 2012. Pop-up retailing: The design, implementation, and five-year evolution of an experiential learning project. *Journal of Marketing Education*, 34(3), pp. 284–296.

Bustamante, J. C. & Rubio, N., 2017. Measuring customer experience in physical retail environments. *Journal of Service Management*, 28(5), pp. 884–913.

Camus, S. & Poulain, M., 2008. La spiritualité: émergence d'une tendance dans la consommation. *Management & Avenir*, 5(19), pp. 72–90.

Carù, A. & Cova, B., 2006. Expériences de consommation et marketing expérientiel. *Revue française de gestion*, 3(162), pp. 93–113.

Chen, W.-C. & Fiore, A. M., 2017. Factors affecting Taiwanese consumers' responses toward pop-up retail. *Asia Pacific Journal of Marketing and Logistics*, 29(2), pp. 370–392.

Comarch Retail Suite, 2018. *Le retail hybrid.* [Online] Available at: www.comarch.fr [Accessed 12 04 2018].

Constantinides, E., 2006. The marketing mix revisited: Towards the 21st century marketing. *Journal of Marketing Management*, 22, pp. 407–438.

CPM experts, 2015. *El marketing experiencial en el punto de venta? que implica?* [Online] Available at: https://cpmexpertus.es/el-marketing-experiencial-en-el-punto-de-venta/ [Accessed 06 02 2018].

CradlePoint, 2012. Trends in pop-up retail: Innovative merchandising driven by flexible, dependable mobile connectivity, s.l.: s.n.

Cramer, Event Marketer, 2017. *Experiential marketing trends.* [Online] Available at: http://cramer.com/experiential-marketing-trends/volume-one/ [Accessed 24 11 2017].

Daucé, B. & Rieunier, S., 2002. Le marketing sensoriel du point de vente. *Recherche et Applications en Marketing*, 17(4), pp. 45–65.

Deloitte, 2014. *Fashion and luxury lookbook,*. s.l.: Deloitte.

Deloitte, 2017. *Global powers of retailing 2017. The art and science of customers.* [Online] Available at: https://www.google.fr/search?q=the+art+and+-science+of+retail+reinvention&oq=the+art+and+science+of+retail+re-invention+&aqs=chrome.69i57.8243j0j4&sourceid=chrome&ie=UTF-8 [Accessed 06 12 2017].

Deprez, L., 2018. *Dada s'installe en pop-up au printemps.* [Online] Available at: FashionNetwork.com [Accessed 06 02 2018].

Deslandes, M., 2018. *Zara teste un pop-up uniquement dédié aux commandes en ligne.* [Online] Available at: FashionNetwork.com [Accessed 05 02 2018].

Edwards, J., 2017. *The most astonishing and predictable trend in economics just got more astonishing and predictable.* [Online] Available at: http://www.businessinsider.fr/uk/online-share-of-retail-economics-2017-12/ [Accessed 05 01 2018].

Filser, M., 2003. La Marketing sensoriel: La quête de l'integration théorique et managériale. *Revue Française du Marketing*, (194), pp. 5–11.

Flambard-Ruaud, S., 1997. Les évolutions du concept marketing. *Décisions Marketing*, 1 Mai-Août, (11), pp. 7–20.

Forbes, 2008. *Pop-up shops: Small stores, big business.* [Online] Available at: https://www.forbes.com/2008/02/01/popup-stores-retail-designers-forbeslife-cx_ls_0201popup.html#14d38a5d7bea [Accessed 11 09 2017].

Foster, J. & McLelland, M. A., 2014. Retail atmospherics: The impact of a brand dictated theme. *Journal of Retailing and Consumer Services*, 22, pp. 195–205.

Fowler, K. & Bridges, E., 2010. Consumer innovativeness: Impact on expectations, perceptions, and choice among retail formats. *Journal of Retailing and Consumer Services*, 17, pp. 492–500.

Frazer, M. & Stiehler, B. E., 2014. *Omnichannel retailing: The merging of the online and off-line environment.* s.l.: s.n., pp. 655–665.

Gentile, C., Spiller, N. & Noci, G., 2007. How to sustain the customer experience: An overview of experience components that co-create value with the custome. *European Management Journal*, 25(5), pp. 395–410.

Germack, D., 2014. *Luxury design.* [Online] Available at: http://www.luxury-design.com/inspiration/pop-up-store-kenzo-haussmann [Accessed 13 11 2017].

Giaimo, A., 2017. *Real estate days.* [Online] Available at: https://media10.simplex.tv/content/73/4448/91335/ [Accessed 11 08 2018].

Guingois, S., 2015. *Pop-up store: Le nouveau format vedette du retail.* [Online] Available at: www.IFLS.net [Accessed 15 04 2018].

Haas, S. & Schmidt, L., 2016. *What drives the success of pop-up stores?* s.l.: Wissenschaftliche Beiträge.

Haas, S. & Schmidt, L., 2016. *What drives the success of pop-up stores?*, s.l.: Technical University of Applied Sciences.

Hansen, K. & Singh, V., 2009. Market structure across retail formats. *Marketing Science*, 28(4), pp. 656–673.

Harel, C., 2016. *Magnum ouvre un bar éphémère au Carrefour de Villiers-en-Bière.* [Online] Available at: https://www.lsa-conso.fr/magnum-ouvre-un-bar-ephemere-au-carrefour-de-villiers-en-biere, 239940 [Accessed 12 02 2018].

Hékimian, A., 2018. *Le pop-up store comme réponse à la crise de l'immobilier commercial.* [Online] Available at: https://www.linkedin.com/pulse/le-pop-up-store-comme-r%C3%A9ponse-%C3%A0-la-crise-de-allison-h%C3%A9kimian?articleId=6368850090035068928#comments-63688-50090035068928&trk=public_profile_article_view [Accessed 09 2019].

Hirschman, E. C. & Holbrook, M. B., 1982. Hedonic consumption: Emerging concepts, Methods and propositions. *Journal of Marketing*, Summer, 46(3), pp. 92–101.

Hughes, C., 2007. Pop-up stores pop in to fill vacancies. *The New York Times*, 05 06.

Influencia, 2017. *Influencia.* [Online] Available at: http://www.influencia.net/fr/actualites/art-culture,luxe, pop-up-store-levier-experientiel-luxe, 7802.html [Accessed 13 11 2017].

InsiderTrends, n.d. *Top 50 innovations in retail.* [Online] Available at: www.insidertrends.com [Accessed 07 01 2018].

Jones, P., Comfort, D. & Hillier, D., 2017. A commentary on pop up shops in the UK. *Property Management*, 35(5), pp. 545–553.

Kim, H., Fiore, A., Niehm, L. & Jeong, M., 2010. Psychographic characteristics affecting behavioral intentions towards pop-up retail. *International Journal of Retail & Distribution Management*, 38(2), pp. 133–154.

KPMG, 2009. *The evolution of retailing. Reinventing the customer experience.* [Online] Available at: us.kpmg.com [Accessed 11 01 2018].

Laparade, O., 2017. *Carcassonne: des boutiques éphémères dans le centre-ville pour Noël.* [Online] Available at: http://www.lindependant.fr/2017/12/21/carcassonne-des-boutiques-ephemeres-dans-le-centre-ville-pour-noel, 3081940.php [Accessed 11 05 2018].

LaVito, A., 2017. *Yankee Candle visits New York for the holidays. Here's why more brands are opening pop-up shops.* [Online] Available at: https://www.cnbc.com/2017/11/22/pop-up-shops-are-becoming-a-new-way-of-heralding-in-the-holidays.html [Accessed 30 11 2017].

Lemoine, J.-F. Jul 2004. *Revue Française du Marketing, Paris*, 198(3/5), pp. 107–116.

Lemoine, J.-F., 2005. L'atmosphère du point de vente comme variable strategique commerciale: Bilan et perspectives. *Décisions Marketing*, Juillet-Septembre, (39), pp. 79–82.

L'indépendant, 2017. *Möbius, l'économie autrement*. s.l.: L'indépendant. Carcassonne.

Liza, 2017. *Le journal du Luxe*. [Online] Available at: https://journalduluxe. fr/pop-up-stores-strategie-marques/ [Accessed 13 11 2017].

Martínez Navarro, G., 2016. *El retail experiencial: un nuevo enfoque en la comunicación de marca*. Madrid-España: Universidad Complutense de Madrid-España.

Monteiro, V. R., 2014. *Pop-up retail as an enhancer of the city brand –A marketing plan for Porto*. Porto: U.Porto Faculdade Do Porto.

Newton, A., 2017. *6 reasons why pop-up stores are excelling*. [Online] Available at: https://retailnext.net/en/blog/6-reasons-why-pop-up-stores-are-excelling/ [Accessed 11 01 2018].

Nicasio, F., 2015. The Meteoric rise of rop-up retail: A look at significant facts and stats around pop-up stores. [Online] Available at: https://blog.vendhq.com/post/64901825337/the-meteoric-rise-of-pop-up-retail-a-look-at-significant-facts-and-stats-around-pop-up-stores [Accessed 17 January 2017].

Niehm, L. S., Ann Marie, F., Jeong, M. & Kim, H.-J., 2007. Pop-up retail's acceptability as an innovative business strategy and enhancer of the consumer shopping experience. *Journal of Shopping Center Research*, 13(7), pp. 1–30.

Ochs, A. & Remy, E., 2006. Marketing stratégique et distribution a l'aune du marketing expérientiel: Porter aux pays des merveilles. *Decisions Marketing*, Avril-Juin, (42), pp. 75–81.

Picot-Coupey, K., 2014. The pop-up store as a foreign operation mode (FOM) for retailers. *International Journal of Retail & Distribution Management*, 42(7), pp. 643–670.

Picot-Coupey, K., n.d. *Pop-up stores*. [Online] Available at: https://www.scoop.it/t/pop-up-stores [Accessed 13 11 2017].

Planchard, C., 2012. *« Les boutiques éphémères »*, *un concept bien parti pour durer*. [Online] Available at: http://www.20minutes.fr/economie/945305-20120601-les-boutiques-ephemeres-concept-bien-parti-durer [Accessed 14 11 2017].

Popup Republic, n.d. Popup republic. [Online] Available at: https://popuprepublic.com/our-services/ [Accessed 01 2017].

Pras, B., 2012. La résilience du marketing. *Revue Française de Gestion*, 9(228/229), pp. 59–85.

PWC, 2017. *2017 Retail and industry trends, showrooms, retail experience and compelling economics*. [Online] Available at: www.strategyand.pwc.com [Accessed 11 01 2018].

Rhee, M. & Mehra, S., 2006. A strategic review of operations and marketing functions in retail banks. *International Journal of Service Industry Management*, 17(4), pp. 364–379.

Rosenthal, F., 2009. *Magasin éphémère, pop-up stores: quelles justifications?* [Online] Available at: http://www.retail-distribution.info/article-magas

Russo Spena, T., Caridà, A., Colurcio, M. & Melia, M., 2012. Store experience and co-creation: The case of temporary shop. *International Journal of Retail & Distribution Management*, 40(1), pp. 21–40.

Savitt, R., 1980. Historical research in marketing. *Journal of Marketing*, Autumn, 44(4), pp. 52–58.

Schmitt, B., 1999. Experiential marketing. *Journal of Marketing Management*, 15, pp. 53–67.

Schwab, P.-N., 2014. *Pop-up stores: ce qu'ils révèlent sur l'avenir du commerce de détail.* [Online] Available at: http://www.intotheminds. com/blog/pop-up-stores-ce-quils-revelent-lavenir-du-commerce-detail/ [Accessed 16 04 2018].

Sénécal, S., 2015. *L'évolution de l'expérience client.* s.l.: HEC Montréal. Les cahiers des leçons inaugurables.

Shilpha, B. & Rajnish, J., 2013. Measuring retail customer experience. *International Journal of Retail & Distribution Management*, 41(10), pp. 790–804.

Slywotzky, A., Christensen, C. M., Tedlow, R. S. & Carr, N. G., 2000. The future of commerce. *Harvard Business Review*, pp. 1–20.

Smajovic, H. & Warfvinge, H., 2014. *Pop-up Stores in Fashion Retailing: A description of temporary retailing in relation to Flagship Stores and Outlet Stores.* s.l.: University of Gothenburg.

Sophelle, Focus Report, 2017. *Boundaryless.* [Online] Available at: https:// www.sophelle.com/focus-report-download-form/ [Accessed 17 11 2017].

Spence, N., Puccinelli, N., Grewal, D. & Roggeveen, A., 2014. Store atmospherics: A multisensory perspective. *Psychology and Marketing*, 31(7), pp. 472–488.

Srinivasan, S. & Srivastava, R., 2010. Creating the futuristic retail experience through experiential marketing: Is it possible? An exploratory study. *Journal of Retail & Leisure Property*, 9(3), pp. 193–199.

Steimer, S., 2017. *The magic of pop-u shop marketing.* [Online] Available at: https://www.ama.org/publications/MarketingNews/Pages/magic-of-pop-up-shop-marketing.aspx [Accessed 11 02 2018].

Storefront, 2017. *How Brit + Co created a pop-up community.* [Online] Available at: http://blog.thestorefront.com/fr/how-brit-co-created-a-pop-up-community/ [Accessed 18 02 2018].

Swedberg, C., 2017. *Pop-up experience brings RFID solution to stores.* [Online] Available at: http://www.rfidjournal.com/articles/view?16495/ [Accessed 08 11 2017].

The Storefront, n.d. *Future of retail desires temporary experiences.* [Online] Available at: http://blog.thestorefront.com/future-of-retail-desires-temporary-experiences/ [Accessed 11 09 2017].

Tomlinson, M., 2014. [Online] Available at: www.business.ee.co.uk

Trendwatching, 2004. Trendwatching. [Online] Available at: http:// trendwatching.com/trends/POPUP_RETAIL.htm [Accessed 07 03 2016].

Wang, J., 2018. The rise of the pop-up economy. *Forbes*, 29 09.

WeArePopup, 2017. *We are pop-up.* [Online] Available at: http://blog.
wearepopup.com/ [Accessed 11 01 2017].

Witkiwski, T. H. & Jones, D. B., 2016. Historical research in marketing:
Literature, knowledge and disciplinary status. *Information and Culture*,
51(3), pp. 401–418.

Yvernault, V., 2016. *Cdiscount ouvre à Paris un espace éphémère pour
faire découvrir son offre de jouets.* [Online] Available at: https://www.
lsa-conso.fr/cdiscount-ouvre-a-paris-un-espace-ephemere-pour-faire-
decouvrir-son-offre-de-jouets,250224 [Accessed 12 02 2018].

2 What are ephemeral stores and how can we define them?

Pop-up stores are heretofore not defined by a single, universally shared interpretation. Throughout the studied texts, interchangeable use of the terms "pop-up stores" and "pop-up shop" is encountered and it signifies "ephemeral stores".

At first, pop-up stores presented innovative alternatives to traditional physical points of sale, dominated by the fundamental precepts of permanent systems (Stephens, 2012). Originally, pop-up stores were "marketing gimmicks" helping brands sell their products in unexpected places that didn't conform to traditional spaces. Then, they associated with "cool" and urban concepts which quickly generated pop-up concepts designed for media appeal or even the chance to face a new market (Burbank, 2017). The concept's development and its various representations gave rise to a multitude of names, terms or expressions. Definitions refer to expressions reflecting a state, approach or utility. As the origin of pop-up stores began in Anglo-Saxon countries, many of the expressions used to describe this phenomenon are found in English (Figure 2.1).

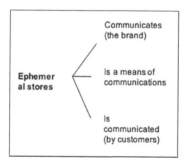

Figure 2.1 Ephemeral store definition

2.1 Managerial definitions of pop-up stores

Pop-up stores are first and foremost "hit-and-run retailing" (Marks & Solan, 2003), appearing in a given place and time, making an impact and disappearing. They are anchored in the present and do not reveal their future actions. The terms "here today; gone tomorrow" or "now you see it; now you don't" (Economist, 2009) affirm the uncertainty of the future (Verheyen, 2017) related to these stores. Pop-ups take people by surprise and encourage them to visit (Newton, 2017) before they disappear, choose to reappear elsewhere or morph into something else.

Not far from the definition of the unforeseen, ephemeral stores are often linked to the concept of "guerilla" (or guerilla marketing) (Wang, 2018[b]); knowing that they do not claim hostility or the creation of disadvantageous activities, rather, this attribution reflects their urban and mischievous side. This trait does not seem to bother consumers and sees only an increase in use among brands. This change in perspective of brand representation (Giaimo, 2017) is expressed by the significant momentum gained, thus helping the transition of retail from a traditional aspect to an innovative aspect.

On the other hand, it has been noticed that brands who used these stores appreciated more and more the "experimental and capricious" approach to retail (Wang, 2018[a]). Technology has contributed to the achievement of a "fluid experience" within pop-up stores, considering consumers and their new habits. Also given the name of "Airbnb of retail" (Stevens, 2017), these "commercial agitators" (Guertchakoff, 2016) introduced new ways of presenting retail formats and gave new meanings to retail; they show how much today's commerce is getting closer and closer to collaborative commerce. Brands are tirelessly in the process of bringing novelty (Newton, 2017) to their concepts and representations to fit in with new trends in consumer behaviour as well as cater to the demands of internet users. Pop-up stores are situated between "online and offline" (Fan, 2016), thus providing a "good compromise".

Pop-up stores are considered as investments in new places (Mayer, 2017) for a temporary period (Burn-Callander, 2015) or a short-term performance (Schwab, 2014; Giaimo, 2017). They are malleable "commerce testers" (Parigi, 2017) and associate well with digital commerce or technologies helping to mobilize the consumer between various brand points of contact (Deslandes, 2018). Different professional sources present a variety of pop-up store explanations (Table 2.1).

Table 2.1 Professional interpretations of pop-up store definitions

Professional interpretations of pop-up store definitions
"Stores that open for a limited time then simply close, and this only to pop up later in another location" (Stephens, 2012).
"Pop-up stores are tools that are easily used by traditional or digital brands, regardless of their size. They have become solutions for acquiring attention and means of improving engagement and loyalty" (Sophelle, 2017).
"The pop-up store is an embodiment of the digital age. It allows brands to perform functions that cannot be met by the digital brand. It intuitively and tangibly embodies the brand's universe, is a new territory of expression that challenges the brand's creativity and offers consumers an intensified experience" (Klépierre, QualiQuanti, 2015).
The pop-up store is defined as "a store that opens in a temporary location and intends to operate only for a short period" (Aubry, Souza, 2011).
"A shop, restaurant, collective of shops or an event that opens quickly in a temporary location and intends to operate only for a short time" (Leinbach-Reyhle, 2014).
"Think of the cookie stands that little Girl Scout run. Think of the sudden appearances of Halloween stores. Pop-up stores are "low-cost", temporary installations that playfully infiltrate the urban landscape; they refer to the common strategies of small traders in villages and towns" (Wang, 2018[a]).
"The pop-up store occupies a space that is vacant for a limited time and can be represented in the form of a restaurant, an art gallery, a boutique or mobile format such as food trucks" (Gobe, 2014).
"The word pop-up denotes a limited lifespan format. The first attempt at a temporary store was to sell limited editions of products and the store was supposed to close after the stock ran out. Today, we distinguish pop-up stores that make sales in a limited period and a new neighbourhood (for commercial purposes) and the most conceptual pop-up stores aimed at reinforcing the brand's value for maximum media coverage" (Schwab, 2014).
"A shop or store set up and open for a relatively short period. Pop-up stores reflect the term 'to pop-up' which describes the appearance of these stores one day and their possible disappearances the next day. The term ephemeral store is also used" (Guingois, n.d.).
"Pop up stores are initiatives that tend to pop up without warning, draw crowds quickly, and then either fade away or morph into something else, adding to retail the fresh feel, exclusivity and surprise" (Trendwatching, 2004).
"Pop-up stores come in three forms. The first form is the ephemeral store; can be a traditional shop, a restaurant, an art gallery. The second form is the pop-up event; a festival, market or concert, and the third, lesser-known form is pop-up planning; this is at the municipal level and as part of the investment of public projects associated with the pop-up" (Gobe, 2014).

2.1.1 Pop-up store objectives and their characteristics

Given their liveliness and flexibility, ephemeral stores have affirmed their place within a multitude of brands which want to reinvent themselves (Martínez Navarro, 2016). As "retail" is not exclusively represented by physical stores, and since digital commerce has marked its strong presence among distribution channels, different cases of online, offline or hybrid brands engaging in pop-up stores are found[1] (Wang, 2018a). There are, however, several trends related to pop-up store presentations: established or mature brands (Pontiroli, 2017), designer or start-up brands, and "pure players" or digital natives (Klépierre, QualiQuanti, 2015) (Clément-Bollée, 2018). Pop-up stores can be an action of an individual brand or an action of a collective of brands pooling efforts (Bouleau, 2017) and presenting themselves in the same place at the same time, whilst each proposes its offer.

2.1.2 Brand objectives

Pop-up stores borrow from traditional marketing, communications and experiential marketing objectives. In the logic of ephemeral commerce, pop-ups are "customer centric" (customer-centred or customer oriented) (KPMG, 2009). Brands are faced with two different possibilities (Crane, 2018) (Sophelle, Focus Report, 2017): the objectives in close relation with the operationalization of the brand on one hand and the objectives concerning the experience that the brand offers to its customers on the other hand. In the case of pop-up stores, the most common brand objectives are expressed by commercial or communication objectives (Elise, 2017).

Thus, brand objectives can be to strengthen (Giaimo, 2017) (Newton, 2017) or increase sales (ESCP Europe, 2017). Profitability is only one of the objectives (Bouleau, 2017) which refer to the commercial aspect; this can be a seasonal operation or a destocking (Elise, 2017) (Schwab, 2014). However, pop-up stores are widely used to test new markets (Giaimo, 2017), or even a product or concept (Deschamps, 2017) (Deslandes, 2018), to bring people in (Laparade, 2017) or to act as point of contact with them (Planchard, 2012). It becomes a presentation of the brand (Samaoui & Jaoued-Abbassi, 2007) which often helps to showcase its style (Terdoslavich, 2017) (CPM experts, 2015) and its history (Fan, 2016).

Brands adopting pop-up stores aim at creating an engagement (Fan, 2016), even an emotional engagement (Martínez Navarro,

2016), by proposing memorable experiences, proposing a shopping experience (Keyes, 2017), "providing consumers with an experience" (Guingois, 2015) or delivering an immersive and unique experience. These "punch" operations are focused on media mentions (Elise, 2017). Pop-up stores also help brands build their notoriety (Holmes, 2017) and/or increase their loyalty (Giaimo, 2017) following an action based on differentiated or "refined" positioning (Elise, 2017).

2.1.3 Characteristics of pop-up stores and their uses

Pop-up stores are characterized by their agility (Newton, 2017), flexibility (The Storefront, n.d.) and mobility (Losif, 2015). That being said, there are no specific steps that require these types of stores managers to operate them. They are "transitional tools" (Schwab, 2014) or "connectors" (Dunn, 2017) that benefit from a "freedom of expression" that is both different and innovative each time.

While promoting (Deschamps, 2017) ideas in-situ, the ephemeral store enters into direct interaction (Schwab, 2014; Steimer, 2017) with consumers. It collects "on-site" information and real-time feedback (Newton, 2017). This link that the brand creates with customers through the pop-up store (Edwards, 2017) (Caussil, 2017) turns into a "buzz" (Steimer, 2017). Pop-up stores are therefore very useful for the brand (Bouleau, 2017; Elise, 2017) as they are part of its strategy and, following very specific objectives (Influencia, 2017), take "body and soul" (Edwards, 2017), come to meet consumers and talk to them on behalf of the brand.

2.1.4 Pop-up store formats, advantages and disadvantages

Pop-up stores find themselves under the retail world's spotlight; they are a "star" retail format (Guingois, 2015) that brands view as a "tool" for contacting customers (Steimer, 2017) (Holmes, 2017). A pop-up store can exist in different shapes and sizes (Retailtouchpoints, n.d.; Shopify, n.d.). There are waves of new formats that delight customers and keep them wanting to explore more. These formats can be physical, digital, event based or project based and are conceived to resurface the retail experience (Brandpos, n.d.). A pop-up store can be best described as a "Swiss Army knife" (Guingois, 2015), a communication medium – going from virtual to real – and an agile format associated with an experiential place (Table 2.2).

The format presentation list may be longer and more developed than the one proposed above; this is due to the nature of ephemeral

Table 2.2 Different pop-up store formats

Among a long list, pop-up stores could appear in one of the following formats (Guingois, 2015; Keyes, 2017; Marciniak & Budnarowska, 2018)

Different pop-up store formats	An art gallery, a theatre, a garden, a train station or an airport. A kiosk or a stand in a shopping centre or a department store (or PUIS: pop-up in-store). A motorized vehicle (Fashion Truck, Food Truck, etc.). A hangar or an inflatable balloon or modular structure. A vacant space at street level; the most popular format so far. The digital world has also developed an interest in the concept of the ephemeral by creating platforms where the message expires or websites qualified as "temporary" and which expire or disappear. Pop-up store formats fill a spectrum that ranges from artistic displays to publicity stunts (Wang, 2018).

stores which manifest differently each time according to the brands' needs and their identity, the context, the time, the period, the place, the consumers, the environment and so on. This "what" (Sophelle, Focus Report, 2017) of the brand occupies different types of commercial spaces (Gobe, 2014), and describes a concept's materialized aspect that the brand wants to highlight.

Despite their innumerable advantages, pop-up stores have some drawbacks. Their attractiveness is the short duration and imprecision of their shelf life. This is one of the advantages that characterizes this type of sale and that makes it so exciting to consumers. It is a tool that communicates the brand promise to consumers (The Storefront, n.d.). A major advantage is the fact that they can be easily assembled or disassembled (Hallisy, 2006; Ryan, 2008), thus allowing new, unconventional and inexpensive ways of physical manifestation, allowing brands to avoid overhead and rental costs (Carapiet, 2009). With pop-up stores, brands can "reach out to customers" and get in closer contact with them. The choice of location helps in getting in touch with the audience that the brand targets and wishes to get in touch with. Such contexts become active sites rather than being passive backdrops (Dean, 2012). To conclude, pop-up stores present low risks and low cost compared to traditional stores (Dunn, 2017) and could be possible momentary solutions to meeting different brand needs.

The drawbacks, however, show that this type of point of sale will not necessarily be able to support a brand's success because of its short duration (Anon., n.d.). Moreover, the impact of these stores may disappear if the concept lasts a long time or if the same concept is repeated several times. Consequently, the brand requires a permanent renewal of the chosen format's concept, its communications and all its operational aspects. From a profit-generation point of view, there is only a short period to be able to generate profits from the specific pop-up store (Firestone, 2006), which might stress brands that are in need of generating quick results or solving problems in a short period of time.

Conceptualizing a pop-up store is not easy either. This type of point of sale, or space, must present novelty and/or attractiveness to the customer. Consequently, the brand will look for a concept, and will arrange it with the appropriate display, the customer journey, the zones and the offering. Thus, a pop-up store can be akin to an event's execution requiring a lot of attention and qualified team members who are knowledgeable, efficient or able to make the right decisions (The Storefront, n.d.).

2.2 Pop-up stores in academic literature

Consumers have become major driving forces in the retail environment as they have the power to influence the brand's offering and highly affect the retail environment (physical or digital). Moreover, they have more power to state where and how they would want to spend time, where and how they would want to search for information or how they would want to influence their purchasing behaviour (Fowler & Bridges, 2010). Brands and consumers are affected and are affecting the changing retail environment (Marciniak & Budnarowska, 2018). This turbulent environment presents new opportunities for brands as well as threats. New technologies and new digital platforms offer new ways of presenting the offer or making it available to consumers. Also, brands have more opportunities to start up through non-traditional and less expensive distribution channels. Although the retail environment offers more possibilities or means for brands, only the brands most empowered to adopt and adapt to these changes and tools will survive.

Customers have also changed. They are now technology savvy, more open to the various online shopping formats – contemporary or traditional – and they are also spending more time online and are connected more than ever. They are becoming more demanding and asking for services that facilitate the search for information and purchasing – innovative formats. They are in continuous movement between different brand touchpoints; they observe, they inject content, they demand content, and according to their means, their time or their desires, they make their choices through a channel, buy on the other and probably will go shopping in a third one (Figure 2.2).

Faced with this situation, consumers affect brands, brands respond to consumers and put forward new formats and tools to meet their everchanging needs. Physical and digital formats overlap and lead brands to rethink commercial strategies that bring them closer to the new reality of commerce; "mobile" commerce (Badot et al., 2018). Pop-up stores are recent forms native to the current retail environment that brands are increasingly adopting. It is a formula that goes from the spatio-temporary principle in the distribution sector and meets the expectations of postmodern consumers. Despite their more extensive uses around the world and by different brands in various industries, they have so far received little academic research, except for a few studies mainly focused on marketing and retail (Pomodoro, 2013).

Ephemeral stores are relatively new formats that appeared out of nowhere and are designed to quickly capture attention and/or purchase dollars, to showcase new product lines and to generate sales and consumer enthusiasm. These are cutting-edge and innovative formats that are characterized by very short lifespans (Fowler &

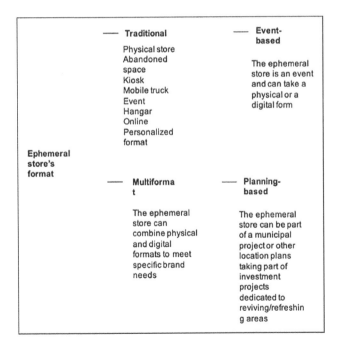

Figure 2.2 Ephemeral store formats

Bridges, 2010). So far, the academic literature does not present a single definition of pop-ups. The most common denomination is "pop-up stores" by analogy with "pop-up windows" on the internet (Kim et al., 2010; De Lassus, 2012; Overdiek, 2017). Furthermore, several nominations are found in professional and academic literature to describe these formats: "short-term storefronts" (Fowler & Bridges, 2010), "temporary shops" (Bagozzi et al., 1991; Burgess, 2012; Russo Spena et al., 2012; Alexander et al., 2018), "itinerant shops" (Picot-Coupey, 2014), "nomadic" stores (or nomad stores) (Alexander et al., 2018), "guerrilla stores" (Picot-Coupey, 2012; Padmalia, 2014; Picot-Coupey, 2014; Edward Spragg, 2017), "experiential stores" (Taube & Warnaby, 2017) (Spitzkat, 2016) or "experiential marketing formats" (Pomodoro, 2013).

"Hyper retail" formats refer to ephemeral stores that have extremely reduced appearance and disappearance cycles (Taube & Warnaby, 2017). Pop-up stores can also be called "flash retailing" (Jones et al., 2017; Alexander et al., 2018). Researchers, however, explain that there is a difference between pop-ups stores and "flash stores": pop-up stores seek to create a superior brand experience, which shows differentiation and generates positive word of mouth (Klein et al., 2016), while "flash" stores are more like seasonal pop-up stores (like Halloween or Christmas stores) (Taube & Warnaby, 2017). Finally, pop-up stores can represent a single brand's project as well as the projects of several brands that unite in a single pop-up store. "Collaborative pop-up stores" are types that bring together several brands and their offers. The same space can accommodate different ephemeral projects simultaneously and, in this case, the form is defined as "shop-sharing" (Alexander et al., 2018). Pop-up stores are also "temporary retail activations" (Lowe et al., 2018), which are a form of brand experience used as an innovative experiential marketing strategy. Such initiatives are based on surprise and exclusivity and aim to engage consumers and strengthen brand loyalty.

After presenting the pop-up stores, and highlighting their characteristics and dependent variables, we present these formats as communications and/or distribution channels. Moreover, we classify pop-up stores and present different objectives that they could help brands meet (Figure 2.3).

2.2.1 Ephemeral store definitions, classifications and dimensions

It is suggested that "true ephemeral stores" use empty or underutilized spaces; have a specific start and end date; do not always aim for

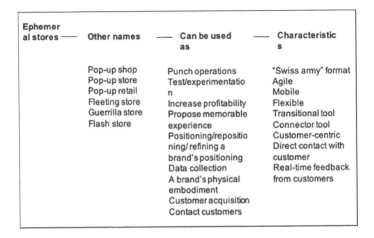

Ephemeral stores ——	Other names ——	Can be used as ——	Characteristics
	Pop-up shop	Punch operations	"Swiss army" format
	Pop-up store	Test/experimentatio	Agile
	Pop-up retail	n	Mobile
	Fleeting store	Increase profitability	Flexible
	Guerrilla store	Propose memorable	Transitional tool
	Flash store	experience	Connector tool
		Positioning/repositio	Customer-centric
		ning/ refining a	Direct contact with
		brand's positioning	customer
		Data collection	Real-time feedback
		A brand's physical	from customers
		embodiment	
		Customer acquisition	
		Contact customers	

Figure 2.3 Ephemeral store characteristics

financial permanence; are designed to be relocated or transferred to another site; and be in some way exclusive, distinct or special (Jones et al., 2017). These are temporary and short-term retail spaces that deliberately arise and then quickly close (Kim et al., 2010; Picot-Coupey, 2014). Pop-up stores, as we know them today, are a relatively new, radical and revolutionary format (Picot-Coupey, 2012). Even though they have sometimes been considered to be very risky (Fowler & Bridges, 2010), these formats are now fully integrated into a brand's strategic mix (Pomodoro, 2013). Similar to any temporary event, ephemeral stores involve people visiting as hosts and participants (Padmalia, 2014; Jones et al., 2017). These stores are opportunities for the brand and the consumer to meet and come closer together (Taube & Warnaby, 2017).

In terms of goals, ephemeral stores don't just focus on breaking even; they combine with communication to stimulate and develop a long-term relationship with consumers that goes beyond direct benefits generation (Picot-Coupey, 2012). Other pop-up adoption goals are introducing new potential customers to the brand, developing relationships with existing customers (Jones et al., 2017) and changing their perceptions of the brand, and providing consumers with a unique experience rather than selling products. As for luxury brands, ephemeral stores allow them to test and strengthen their brand's image in new markets. There are multiple players, each with different perspectives and goals when it comes to experiencing temporary retail activations (Lowe et al., 2018). Ephemeral store concepts have been found to potentially contribute to the achievement of a range of broader business objectives (Taube & Warnaby, 2017) in terms of the following dimensions:

- Communicational (increase awareness or improve the perception of brand values)
- Experiential (facilitate consumer engagement with brands and create brand communities)
- Transactional (increase sales and market share)
- Testing (as a low-risk means of obtaining market information) (Alexander et al., 2018)
- Sale (Chen & Fiore, 2017) (a common way to promote and sell consumer products, in the short term)
- Loyalty (Kim et al., 2010; Chen & Fiore, 2017) (build customer-brand relationship and long-term loyalty)
- For consumers, the goals achieved through temporary retail activations seem to differ and instead focus on novelty, exclusivity, surprise and discovery (Lowe et al., 2018).

Ephemeral store objectives can also go beyond the sole aim of generating direct profits (Picot-Coupey, 2014). In addition to communicating a brand, pop-up stores reinforce its notoriety (Alexander et al., 2018). They aim to generate demand rather than income. For that, pop-up stores offer experiential environments (Kim et al., 2010), help build branding and attract attention and new customers. In the case of luxury brands (Klein et al., 2016), the objective is to stimulate word of mouth to multiply the brand's reach to new target consumers and new points of contact.

When comparing pop-up stores to flagship stores, the following dimensions have been highlighted as characterizing pop-up stores (Smajovic & Warfvinge, 2014): the environment (unique and multi-sensory); merchandise selection and price (new collections, unique products, reasonable prices); location (unforeseen or mobile); and the retail strategy (test of new markets/distribution channels, customer relationship, brand image).

Pop-ups are short-term stores that deliberately set up and close quickly or have limited life cycles. They are open for a short period which can range from a few days to weeks (Klein et al., 2016) up to a year (De Lassus, 2012; Picot-Coupey, 2012; De Lassus & Freire, 2014). They can be reflected through several formats: static formats, such as boutiques, galleries, cafes, bars (Jones et al., 2017) and malls (pop-up mall) (Alexander et al., 2018), or more mobile formats, such as buses, equipped vehicles, stands, market stalls or kiosks (Pomodoro, 2013; De Lassus & Freire, 2014). The choice of the pop-up store format is directly linked to the objective the brand wishes to achieve (Alexander et al., 2018). They position themselves between the virtual and the traditional format: they materialize the concepts of virtual brands through physical representations on the one hand and build links between traditional representations and digital commerce on the other hand (Boustani, 2020).

Locations where pop-up stores appear are both experiential and promotional, showcasing a limited number of products or presenting unique events. They allow visitors to live a unique, personalized and time-limited experience with a brand and its products (De Lassus, 2012) (Kim et al., 2010): "An ephemeral store's location is part of the packaging and the store itself becomes the product consumed" (Alexander et al., 2018).

A brand can choose to pop-up in "trendy" and economically important cities; places based on specific marketing objectives (such as a famous avenue) (Alexander et al., 2018); or in radical, little-known (Picot-Coupey, 2012; Picot-Coupey, 2014) or other unconventional places (Overdiek, 2017). In the first case, the pop-up store is set up in high-traffic or highly frequented places (popping in department stores) (Alexander et al., 2018). In the second case, the pop-up store can be installed in old metro stations, abandoned buildings or other similar locations. In the context of pop-up stores, a place is a criterion that helps brands to strengthen their reputations and help them be "reinvented or created" (Alexander et al., 2018; Boustani, 2020). Three roles of ephemeral stores appear in the international localization strategy: characteristics, forms and function (Alexander et al., 2018).

Ephemeral stores are means of brand classifications. They help less established brands overcome potential difficulties in securing space in established retail channels (Overdiek, 2017; Tansel, 2017). A pop-up store format can also be adopted by these brands to obtain maximum visibility and test the market without a huge financial investment (Pomodoro, 2013). On the other hand, for the more established brands, pop-up stores aim to increase their image, promote new collections or limited editions (Alexander et al., 2018), or test new, international or strategic markets (Pomodoro, 2013). They offer new possibilities for luxury brands (Taube & Warnaby, 2017) to present their customers or targeted audience "a more accessible and less formal way" to the brand. For online brands (pure players), pop-up stores offer possibilities and opportunities to add a physical experience (offline experience) for their consumers to experience new products and services (Overdiek, 2017).

Ephemeral stores are means to a specific brand's end. Whether it is through events, customer engagement, brand/customer interaction or through distribution channels, they serve their purpose and meet brand strategic objectives.

- A means of communication focused on events: From a functional perspective, pop-up stores are perceived as a means of event communication (or a marketing communication method) (Picot-Coupey, 2012) because they are largely supported by communications in the press or in blogs (De Lassus, 2012). They are considered the "latest expression of innovative solutions" in marketing channels. Pop-up stores are supported by new technologies and promotional activities to facilitate an interactive consumer experience (Taube & Warnaby, 2017). They are event-driven, they create a "buzz" (Alexander et al., 2018) and a sense of urgency (*I must see; I must have*), and they also stimulate purchasing behaviour or other action (Taube & Warnaby, 2017) (Chen & Fiore, 2017) (Marciniak & Budnarowska, 2018). Consumers are now interweaving physical and virtual channels in their shopping behaviour. The "smartphone" encourages mobile users to visit a store and can then help them integrate into the store experience. Using the smartphone, consumers can easily access information, about the brand before entering the pop-up store, during the visit or after they leave the pop-up store. Consumers can also access other brand touchpoints if they are willing pursue their shopping experience (Picot-Coupey, 2013).
- An interactive platform: Pop-up stores are defined as an "interactive and relational platform" that activate content and meaning through multi-sensory customer engagement (Kim et al., 2010; Russo Spena et al., 2012; Picot-Coupey, 2014). Consumer and brand roles are now mixed: exchanges and interactions in a pop-up store shape and transform the brand's offer and/or decisions (Kim et al., 2010).
- A means of distribution: Pop-up stores are also a new form of distribution that can prove to be very successful (De Lassus, 2012) on its own as well as a complement to other distribution channels (especially online channels) (Gibbs, 2016); most importantly, it is developed in synergy with other temporary events and initiatives. Pop-up stores are "a kind of synthesis between communication and sales" (Picot-Coupey, 2012; Picot-Coupey, 2014).

As previously mentioned, three pop-up store dimensions (Alexander et al., 2018) have been highlighted: form, functions and characterizing traits. Form encompasses all the appearances that pop-up stores can take. Function relates to awareness, promotion, engagement, relationships, new product launches and collaborations. Finally, among the features that characterize pop-up stores are its limited duration, its surprise effect, the new products they offer, the imaginative aspect, exclusivity, the specific aspect of the place or flexibility. Ephemeral store dimensions could also relate to experiential, artistic and social ones.

- An experiential marketing dimension: Store-specific characteristics are intrinsic to experiential retail in general and pop-up stores in particular (Klein et al., 2016). Pop-up stores are considered a new experiential marketing format (Taube & Warnaby, 2017) (Picot-Coupey, 2012; Pomodoro, 2013; Picot-Coupey, 2014) based on surprise and exclusivity and are intended to engage or to involve (Picot-Coupey, 2014) consumers. They create brand experiences and increase word-of-mouth sharing among existing and new target consumer groups simultaneously (Taube & Warnaby, 2017).
- An artistic dimension: Ephemeral store atmospheres reveal a theatrical character and can be imagined as an artistic format (Picot-Coupey, 2012). Pop-up stores provide an attractive store atmosphere and a unique retail environment. Their atmospheric design is usually welcoming and interactive and makes it easier for consumers to access the brand (Klein et al., 2016). This temporary space also provides the opportunity to experiment with innovative solutions to create not only a space to exhibit and be admired but also an interactive space capable of telling stories, creating shared experiences (Russo Spena et al., 2012), "aesthetic experiences" (Monteiro, 2014), and offering surprising and exciting experiences (Alexander et al., 2018).
- A social dimension: The social dimension of an ephemeral store's atmosphere is highlighted both by the physical design of the social space and by the use of multimedia tools, which simultaneously connect with other points of contact (for example, virtual communities, radio, television and the internet) to allow a better resonance with the customer experience (Russo Spena et al., 2012).

Ephemeral store popularity is due to the traits characterizing this format. They correspond to the new modern or the postmodern economy described by Firat and Venkatesh (1993) as they are based on surprise, exclusivity and discovery and how they facilitate the creation of experiences (Picot-Coupey, 2012). They are also characterized by their ability to reflect the brand's identity to target customers in a given location and for a limited time (Taube & Warnaby, 2017; Boustani, 2020). As a consequence of the temporary specificity of ephemeral stores, they are characterized by their ability help brands innovate and improvise (Picot-Coupey, 2012).

An ephemeral store can also be viewed as a distribution format with distinctive hedonic traits. That being said, it can be considered in itself as a medium: it is a way to educate consumers, to trigger word-of-mouth communication or to amplify sharing on social networks. Also known as "guerilla stores", it can follow "guerilla marketing" techniques in order to deliver a coherent and distinctive message (Picot-Coupey, 2012) by deploying a communication mix plan or by heavily relying on "storytelling" (Tansel, 2017). As an "interactive and narrative place", ephemeral stores allow brands to market themselves; to share information regarding customers on different aspects such as production, technology and risks; and to offer real access to an "extraordinary brand experience" (Russo Spena et al., 2012).

These stores offer interactive environments to meet the current postmodern consumer needs (Picot-Coupey, 2012) and to feed their attractiveness to the hedonic advantages associated with the novelty of these formats, rather than utilitarian advantages such as facilitating decision-making. They can also be interpreted as "a trendy and hypermodern platform" focusing on a generation of consumer seeking new experiences and subject to ad hoc decision-making (Overdiek, 2017). Ephemeral stores give developed or developing brands the flexibility to present their concepts, to test them or to test new ranges of products. These formats are therefore considered as experimental bases that are inexpensive and engaging and which must generate buzz and excitement which is integral to their appeal (Jones et al., 2017).

Note

1 (1) **Savic (2015)**; http://www.rudebaguette.com/2015/12/07/etsy-reopens-pop-up-store-in-paris-for-the-holidays/ (2) **Laura (2016)**; https://www.lebonbon.fr/paris/deco-et-design/zagatub-pop-up-store-start-up-francaises-connectees-decembre-paris/ (3) **Caroline J. (2017)**; https://www.sortiraparis.com/loisirs/shopping-Fashion/articles/153060-nouvelles-scenes-a-paris-pop-up-store-par-previly-et-nestore (4) **Le Popup store Etsy by Ety**; https://www.paperblog.fr/8097195/le-pop-up-store-etsy-by-etsy-toulouse/ (5) **Occitanie Tribune**; http://www.occitanie-tribune.com/articles/5238/herault-montpellier-a-montpellier-un-pop-up-store-unique-26-createurs-a-decouvrir/ (Accessed 13/11/2017).

References

Alexander, B., Nobbs, K. & Varley, R., 2018. The growing permanence of pop-up outlets within the international location strategies of fashion retailers. *International Journal of Retail & Distribution Management*, 46(5), pp. 487–506.

Anon., n.d. Shopify. [Online] Available at: www.shopify.com/guides/ultimate-guide-to-pop-up-shops/marketing-your-pop-up-pt-1[Accessed 09 03 2016].

Aubry, F. & Souza, R., 2011. *The art and science of retail reinvention.* [Online] Available at: https://www.bcg.com/documents/file86012.pdf [Accessed 06 12 2017].

Badot, O., Lemoine, J.-F. & Ochs, A., 2018. *Distribution 4.0.* 1st ed. s.l.: Pearson.

Bagozzi, R. Y., Yi, Y. & Philips, L. W., 1991. Assessing validity construct in organizational research. *Administrative Science Quarterly*, 36, pp. 421–458.

Bouleau, M.-S., 2017. *Le figaro.* [Online] Available at: http://www.lefigaro.fr/sortir-paris/2017/04/12/30004-20170412ARTFIG00048-my-pop-up-store-createur-de-magasins-ephemeres-sur-mesure.php [Accessed 13 11 2017].

Boustani, G., 2020. *Ephemeral store adoption by brands.* Paris: International Marketing Trends Conference.

Brandpos, n.d. *3 tendencias en ka exoeriencia de compra en el punto de venta.* [Online] Available at: http://www.brandpos.com/tendencias-experiencia-de-compra-punto-de-venta/ [Accessed 13 11 2018].

Burbank, J. D., 2017. *Why ecommerce companies love pop-up stores.* [Online] Available at: http://www.tgdaily.com/enterprise/why-ecommerce-companies-love-pop-up-stores [Accessed 17 09 2017].

Burgess, B., 2012. Pop-up retailing: the design, implementation, and five-year evolution of an experiential learning project. *Journal of Marketing Education*, 34(3), pp. 284–296.

Burn-Callander, R., 2015. *The third of UK start-up....* [Online] Available at: http://www.telegraph.co.uk/finance/newsbysector/retailandconsumer/11644470/Third-of-new-UK-start-ups-will-be-pop-up-shops.html [Accessed 17 11 2017].

Carapiet, L., 2009. Pop-up shops quite the fashion. [Online] Available at: www.lexisnexis.com (The Australian Financial Review) [Accessed 30 04 2009].

Caussil, J., 2017. *Boulanger ouvre deux magasins éphémères à Italie 2 et Vélizy 2.* [Online] Available at: https://www.lsa-conso.fr/boulanger-ouvre-deux-magasins-ephemeres-a-italie-2-et-velizy-2,262987 [Accessed 11 02 2018].

Chen, W.-C. & Fiore, A. M., 2017. Factors affecting Taiwanese consumers' responses toward pop-up retail. *Asia Pacific Journal of Marketing and Logistics*, 29(2), pp. 370–392.

Clément-Bollée, B., 2018. *What's in store for the future of retail? Physical storefronts with digital touchpoints.* [Online] Available at: http://blog.thestorefront.com/whats-in-store-for-the-future-of-retail-physical-storefronts-with-digital-touchpoints/ [Accessed 16 04 2018].

CPM experts, 2015. *El marketing experiencial en el punto de venta ? que implica ?* [Online] Available at: https://cpmexpertus.es/el-marketing-experiencial-en-el-punto-de-venta/ [Accessed 06 02 2018].

Crane, A., 2018. Brandless' *'Pop-Up With Purpose' Focuses on Community Over Product.* [Online] Available at: https://mail.google.com/mail/u/0/#inbox/163f32d31ce59823 [Accessed 07 08 2018].

Dean, W., 2012. independent.co.uk. [Online] Available at: http://www.independent.co.uk/news/uk/this-britain/the-pop-up-paradigm-they-may-not-last-for-long-but-temporary-shops-are-here-to-stay-6294576.html [Accessed 14 03 2016].

De Lassus, C., 2012. Les pop-up stores de luxe : entre lieu mythique et endroit éphémère, une analyse sémiotique. *Colloque Etienne Thil*, Lille, France, Oct.

De Lassus, C. & Freire, A., 2014. Acess to luxury brand myth in pop-up stores: A netnographic and semiotic analysis. *Journal of Retailing and Customer Services*, 21, pp. 61–68.

Deschamps, F., 2017. *Amazon va ouvrir un bar éphémère à Tokyo.* [Online] Available at: https://www.lsa-conso.fr/amazon-va-ouvrir-un-bar-ephemere-a-tokyo, 268412 [Accessed 12 02 2018].

Deslandes, M., 2018. *Zara teste un pop-up uniquement dédié aux commandes en ligne.* [Online] Available at: FashionNetwork.com [Accessed 05 02 2018].

Dunn, P., 2017. *The newest pop-up space in Midtown helps entrepreneurs test their businesses, together.* [Online] Available at: http://www.modeldmedia.com/features/cass-collective-popup-042417.aspx [Accessed 08 11 2017].

Economist, 2009. Gone tomorrow. [Online] Available at: http://www.economist.com/business/finance/displaystory.cf,?storyid=14101585&fsrc=rss [Accessed 20 August 2009].

Edward Spragg, J., 2017. Articulating the fashion product life-cycle. *Journal of Fashion Marketing and Management: An International Journal*, 21(4), pp. 499–511.

Edwards, J., 2017. *The most astonishing and predictable trend in economics just got more astonishing and predictable.* [Online] Available at: http://www.businessinsider.fr/uk/online-share-of-retail-economics-2017-12/ [Accessed 05 01 2018].

Elise, 2017. *Welcome to the Jungle.* [Online] Available at: https://www.welcometothejungle.co/articles/mode-pourquoi-les-pop-up-stores-seduisent-les-marques [Accessed 13 11 2017].

ESCP Europe, 2017. *La co-construction de l'expérience.* [Online] Available at: http://www.escpeurope.eu/nc/media-news/news-newsletter/news-single/article/la-co-construction-de-lexperience-shopping-a-lere-de-leconomie-collaborative-et-numerique/ [Accessed 11 08 2017].

Fan, J., 2016. *StroreFront.* [Online] Available at: https://www.across-magazine.com/clash-brick-mortar-click-order-popups-happy-compromise/#.WjKAhOu6chI.linkedin [Accessed 13 12 2017].

Firat, A. & Venkatesh, A., 1993. Postmodernity: The age of marketing. *International Journal of Research in Marketing*, 10(3), pp. 227–249.

Firestone, B. M., 2006. Here today, gone tomorrow! [Online] Available at: www.dramatispersonae.org/student work [Accessed 10 05 2009].

Fowler, K. & Bridges, E., 2010. Consumer innovativeness: Impact on expectations, perceptions, and choice among retail formats. *Journal of Retailing and Consumer Services*, 17, pp. 492–500.

Giaimo, A., 2017. *Real estate days.* [Online] Available at: https://media10. simplex.tv/content/73/4448/91335/ [Accessed 11 08 2018].

Gibbs, P., 2016. What is a shop? Evolution of the retail store. *Operations Management*, 2, pp. 24–26.

Gobe, S. K., 2014. *The pop-up economy.* [Online] Available at: www.dvrpc. org [Accessed 19 02 2018].

Guertchakoff, S., 2016. *Bilan (sur les pop-up stores).* [Online] Available at: http://www.bilan.ch/entreprises-archives/pop-stores-gagnent-terrain-0 [Accessed 13 11 2017].

Guingois, S., 2015. *Pop-up store: Le nouveau format vedette du retail.* [Online] Available at: www.IFLS.net [Accessed 15 04 2018].

Hallisy, B., 2006. *Taking it to the streets: Steps to an effective- and ethical-guerilla marketing campaign.* Tactics, p. 13.

Holmes, N., 2017. *Pop-ups: An essential part of the modern retail strategy.* [Online] Available at: http://www.jllrealviews.com/industries/pop-ups-an-essential-part-of-the-modern-retail-strategy/ [Accessed 08 11 2017].

Influencia, 2017. *Influencia.* [Online] Available at: http://www.influencia. net/fr/actualites/art-culture, luxe, pop-up-store-levier-experientiel-luxe, 7802.html [Accessed 13 11 2017].

Jones, P., Comfort, D. & Hillier, D., 2017. A commentary on pop up shops in the UK. *Property Management*, 35(5), pp. 545–553.

Keyes, D., 2017. *Marie Claire and Mastercard team up to revolutionize the brick-and-mortar experience.* [Online] Available at: http://www. businessinsider.fr/us/marie-claire-and-mastercard-revolutionize-brick-and-mortar-experience-2017-9/ [Accessed 15 11 2017].

Kim, H., Fiore, A., Niehm, L. & Jeong, M., 2010. Psychographic characteristics affecting behavioral intentions towards pop-up retail. *International Journal of Retail & Distribution Management*, 38(2), pp. 133–154.

Klein, J. F., Falk, T., Esch, F.-R. & Gloukhovtsev, A., 2016. Linking pop-up brand stores to brand experience and word of mouth: The case of luxury retail. *Journal of Business Research*, 69(12), pp. 5761–5767.

Klépierre, QualiQuanti, 2015. *Pop-up stores. La conquête d'un territoire d'expression pour les marques.* [Online] Available at: http://www. klepierre.com/content/uploads/2016/02/Livre_Blanc_Pop-up_Store1. pdf [Accessed 17 11 2017].

KPMG, 2009. *The evolution of retailing. Reinventing the customer experience.* [Online] Available at: us.kpmg.com [Accessed 11 01 2018].

Laparade, O., 2017. *Carcassonne : des boutiques éphémères dans le centre-ville pour Noël.* [Online] Available at: http://www.lindependant. fr/2017/12/21/carcassonne-des-boutiques-ephemeres-dans-le-centre-ville-pour-noel,3081940.php [Accessed 11 05 2018]

Laura, 2016. *Zagatub.* [Online] Available at: https://www.lebonbon. fr/paris/deco-et-design/zagatub-pop-up-store-start-up-francaises-connectees-decembre-paris/ [Accessed 13 11 2017].

Leinbach-Reyhle, N., 2014. *Pop-up retailers: Must know details to make yours a success.* [Online] Available at: https://www.forbes.com/sites/ nicoleleinbachreyhle/2014/12/24/pop-up-retailers-must-know-details-to-make-yours-a-success/#7ca69b6127e1 [Accessed 11 01 2018].

Losif, R., 2015. *Le phénomène des pop up stores, parti pour durer?* [Online] Available at: https://viuz.com/2015/10/29/le-phenomene-des-pop-up-stores-parti-pour-durer/?trk=pulse-det-art_view_ext [Accessed 17 03 2016].

Lowe, J., Maggioni, I. & Sands, S., 2018. Critical success factors of temporary retail activations: A multi-actor perspective. *Journal of Retailing and Consumer Services*, 40, pp. 175–185.

Marciniak, R. & Budnarowska, C., 2018. *Exploration of pop-up retail: The department store perspective.* Belgium, 4th International colloquium on design, branding and marketing (ICDBM).

Marks, J. & Sloan, C., 2003. Hit-and-run retailing. *Home Textiles Today*, 01 12.

Martínez Navarro, G., 2016. *El retail experiencial: un nuevo enfoque en la comunicación de marca.* Madrid-España: Universidad Complutense de Madrid-España.

Mayer, M., 2017. *The retail evolution.* [Online] [Accessed 29 10 2017].

Monteiro, V. R., 2014. *Pop-up retail as an enhancer of the city brand –A marketing plan for Porto.* Porto: U.Porto Faculdade Do Porto.

Newton, A., 2017. *6 reasons why pop-up stores are excelling.* [Online] Available at: https://retailnext.net/en/blog/6-reasons-why-pop-up-stores-are-excelling/ [Accessed 11 01 2018].

Overdiek, A., 2017. Fashionnable interventions: The pop-up store as a differential space. *Organizational Aesthetics*, 6(1), pp. 116–134.

Padmalia, M., 2014. The strategy of online start-up business expansion through pop-up stores innovation. *Manajemen & Bisnis Berkala Ilmiah*, 13(1), pp. 215–231.

Parigi, J., 2017. *Des nouveaux testeurs de commerce éphémères et itinérants à Paris.* [Online] Available at: https://www.lsa-conso.fr/des-nouveaux-testeurs-de-commerce-ephemeres-et-itinerants-a-paris, 274857 [Accessed 11 02 2018].

Picot-Coupey, K., 2012. Pop-up stores and the international development of retail networks. *International marketing trends conference*, Venice, Jan.

Picot-Coupey, K., 2013. Les voies d'avenir du magasin physique à l'heure du commerce connecté. *Gestion*, 38(2), pp. 51–61.

Picot-Coupey, K., 2014. The pop-up store as a foreign operation mode (FOM) for retailers. *International Journal of Retail & Distribution Management*, 42(7), pp. 643–670.

Planchard, C., 2012. *« Les boutiques éphémères »*, *un concept bien parti pour durer*. [Online] Available at: http://www.20minutes.fr/economie/945305-20120601-les-boutiques-ephemeres-concept-bien-parti-durer [Accessed 14 11 2017].

Pomodoro, S., 2013. Temporary retail in fashion system: An explorative study. *Journal of Fashion Marketing and Management: An International Journal*, 17(3), pp. 341–352.

Pontiroli, T., 2017. *Stratégies*. [Online] Available at: http://www.strategies.fr/actualites/marques/1055480W/les-pop-up-stores-en-plein-essor.html [Accessed 13 11 2017].

Retailtouchpoints, n.d. www.retailtouchpoints.com/features. [Online] Available at: www.retailtouchpoints.com/features/special-reports/pop-up-stores-become-more-than-just-a-trend [Accessed 02 02 2016].

Russo Spena, T., Caridà, A., Colurcio, M. & Melia, M., 2012. Store experience and co-creation: The case of temporary shop. *International Journal of Retail & Distribution Management*, 40(1), pp. 21–40.

Ryan, J., 2008. Retail week. [Online] Available at: http://www.retail-week.com/stores/retailings-bit-of-rough/5007452.article [Accessed 26 10 2009].

Samaoui, L. & Jaoued-Abbassi, L., 2007. *Impact de la vitrine du point de vente sur les réactions des consommateurs : une étude exploratoire*. [Online] Available at: https://hal-upec-upem.archives-ouvertes.fr/hal-01128169/document [Accessed 11 02 2018].

Savic, D., 2015. *Etsy*. [Online] Available at: http://www.rudebaguette.com/2015/12/07/etsy-reopens-pop-up-store-in-paris-for-the-holidays/ [Accessed 13 11 2017].

Schwab, P.-N., 2014. *Pop-up stores: ce qu'ils révèlent sur l'avenir du commerce de détail*. [Online] Available at: http://www.intotheminds.com/blog/pop-up-stores-ce-quils-revelent-lavenir-du-commerce-detail/ [Accessed 16 04 2018].

Shopify, n.d. Shopify.com/guides/HowToPickThePerfectLocation. [Online] Available at: www.shopify.com/guides/ultimate-guide-to-pop-up-shops/how-to-pick-the-perfect-location [Accessed 09 03 2016]

Smajovic, H. & Warfvinge, H., 2014. *Pop-up Stores in Fashion Retailing: A description of temporary retailing in relation to Flagship Stores and Outlet Stores*. s.l.: University of Gothenburg.

Sophelle, Focus Report, 2017. *Boundaryless*. [Online] Available at: https://www.sophelle.com/focus-report-download-form/ [Accessed 17 11 2017].

Spitzkat, A., 2016. *Here today, gone tomorrow. Consumer experiences at fashion pop-up sales*. s.l.: Lund University.

Steimer, S., 2017. *The magic of pop-u shop marketing*. [Online] Available at: https://www.ama.org/publications/MarketingNews/Pages/magic-of-pop-up-shop-marketing.aspx [Accessed 11 02 2018].

Stephens, D., 2012. *The future is temporary: Retailing in a pop-up world*. [Online] Available at: http://www.retailprophet.com/blog/store-experience/the-future-is-temporary/ [Accessed 11 09 2017].

Stevens, B., 2017. *The rise of pop-up shops and what it means for retail.* [Online] Available at: https://www.retailgazette.co.uk/blog/2017/04/the-rise-and-rise-of-pop-up-shops-and-what-it-means-for-retail/ [Accessed 17 11 2017].

Tansel, U., 2017. Licensors and retailers increasingly experiment with the "pop-up" store model in licensing. *Euromonitor International,* pp. 1–2.

Taube, J. & Warnaby, G., 2017. How brand interaction in pop-up shops influences consumers' perceptions of luxury fashion retailers. *Journal of Fashion Marketing and Management: An International Journal,* 21(3), pp. 385–399.

Terdoslavich, W., 2017. *Pop-up stores are getting smarter.* [Online] Available at: http://www.dmnews.com/e-commerce/pop-up-stores-are-getting-smarter/article/645020/ [Accessed 17 09 2017].

Trendwatching, 2004. Trendwatching. [Online] Available at: http://trendwatching.com/trends/POPUP_RETAIL.htm [Accessed 07 03 2016].

Verheyen, G., 2017. *Instant Glam (Glamour).* [Online] Available at: http://www.glamourparis.com/mode/news/articles/vestiaire-collective-ouvre-un-pop-up-store-a-paris/57055 [Accessed 13 11 2017].

Wang, J., 2018[a]. The rise of the pop-up economy. *Forbes,* 29 09.

Wang, E., 2018[b]. *The origins of pop-up shops.* s.l.: Zady.

3 Somewhere between communications and distributions

Categorizing ephemeral stores

Pop-up stores are changing the facets of commerce: "how owners of commercial buildings rent their spaces; how big brands launch new products; how celebrities promote themselves; and how e-merchants market the goods they sell online" (Jones et al., 2017). However, the retail environment has been changing since ancient times, and all practices that might seem like causing disturbance could only be viewed as a natural evolution of retail and its practices. It has been noted that the Magna Graecia period (600–300 BCE) saw some of the most important cultural and economic developments in ancient European history. The region was considered to be one of the major trading centres of the ancient world and one of the regions where retail marketing was established or, at least, first recorded. History shows an early example of forms of commerce moving from temporary places in the main squares of city centres to more permanent and stable places (Pantano & Dennis, 2017).

3.1 The retail environment undergoing a metamorphosis

Temporary stores have been around for a very long time. Indeed, they existed for decades if not centuries. The first temporary stores were developed by our ancestors who carried out the sale from market stalls to liquidate their surplus items in the city markets. Later on, ice cream and fish-and-chip vans, or even street vendors, could be defined under the category of pop-up stores (Marciniak & Budnarowska, 2018). Retail brands made fundamental advancements in retail practices, possibly due to developments in response to market trends and technological advancement. These practices are evolving in terms of the atmospheric physical or virtual format designs; the offer and service proposition; and the accessibility to different retail formats (Pantano & Dennis, 2017).

The British Council for Shopping Centres published a study called "Empty Shops" which investigated the high rate of vacant stores beginning in the late 1990s. This study explained that the cost of maintaining empty premises has become very high and the owners of these premises were being pressured to lower rental prices. Besides, it has been explained that the image of empty stores in a market or country is one of the most powerful indicators of the pressure retailers go through to survive under current business conditions. In the UK, deeper structural economic problems are behind high vacancy retail rates. Three "structural forces" have been put forward, namely the gradual increase in online shopping; the long-term and cumulative effects of competition from outside and sales taking place in shopping areas / outside the city centre; and finally, the rise of the culture of convenience (Jones et al., 2017). These forces have caused profound changes in city centres and main commercial streets.

A competitive environment leads retailers to create, modify or delete existing retail formats, which leads to a diversification of the retail model development (Miotto & Gomes Parente, 2015). Moreover, the evolution of retail is driven by changing consumer demand and challenges to traditional commerce such as malls and downtown shopping districts. New formats for consumer-engaging retail centres, one-stop shopping, outdoor markets and regional hubs are attracting more consumers (Niehm et al., 2007). The modernization of retail and distribution channels is a broader evolutionary phenomenon linked to the context and, in emerging countries, differs in many ways from the development of Western retail. In emerging countries, more traditional formats tend to be gradually replaced by more efficient forms of modern retail. However, no clear boundaries are separating "organized" retail from traditional or "unorganized" commerce (Miotto & Gomes Parente, 2015).

What seems more relevant in the case of modern retail is its more competitive "multi-line" formats, larger assortment, clean environment and modern facilities that are used to equip it. Consequently, when comparing organized commerce to unorganized commerce, the first type refers to "efficient" formats, such as supermarkets, self-service formats, chain stores and multichannel retailers. As for unorganized commerce, it includes street vendors, small old-fashioned stores and individual units, generally aimed at low-income consumers (Miotto & Gomes Parente, 2015). With the internet's advent and new technologies, retail has radically transformed; new models and new logics have emerged and expanded to encompass organized as well as unorganized brands. E-commerce giants (such as Amazon and Alibaba) strongly influence today's competitive environment (Hagberg et al., 2016).

Yet while e-commerce is a central aspect of digitization, the implications of digitization extend far beyond it. While there are examples of brick-and-mortar stores in crisis and decline due to increased competition from e-commerce providers and new digital retail logic, the absolute majority of sales still and will continue to be carried out in physical stores. Furthermore, many consumers remain devoted to the "real experiences" (Picot-Coupey, 2013) lived in physical stores. There are also examples of new retail formats and adjustments in retail (Hagberg et al., 2016); these concepts reinforce the role of the physical store in the digital age.

More recently, physical stores are impacting digital stores and are being impacted by digitalization. Many online retailers (e-merchants) are implementing new physical store concepts to complement their online activities (Hagberg et al., 2016; Overdiek, 2017). As the omnichannel concept that is becoming mainstream in the retail landscape, pop-up stores are strengthening their locations more than ever and seeing themselves as a key part in the assembly of distribution channels (Hagberg et al., 2016). Physical commerce is currently designed in a logic of digital integration and sees digital devices increasingly populating its stores. These "devices" are also supplied by retailers or worn by hyper-connected consumers (Hagberg et al., 2016) who are in possession of a smartphone, a tablet or a computer and have the possibility to buy any product at any time (Picot-Coupey, 2013).

It is only in recent years that social science research has become involved in narratives of "mobility, fluidity, liquidity". Research has shifted from static structures to the "liquefaction" of social structures and/or institutions; a transition from heavy and solid modernity to a "liquid, amorphous and fluid" modernity. In this society, the transient environment produces an attachment to the rapid renewal of everything, to the continuous desire for new objects to be admired and consumed momentarily. As a result, "mobility, liquidity and ephemeral nature" generate an obsession with novelty among consumers (Pomodoro, 2013; Badot et al., 2018).

Contemporary consumers seek to live "temporary experiences" or "portions of experiences". They organize their lives around consumption guided by seduction and volatile cravings. This social tendency underlies the obsession with time, especially the present tense. Guided by the ethics of "carpe diem", postmodern consumers are stimulated by a search for urgent, immediate and prompt gratification. For instance, a postmodern lifestyle emphasizes the importance of the present time, a time perceived as euphoric, and it denies any concern for the future. The authors Bauman (2000) and Lipovetsky (2004) both emphasize new consumer realities that are more liquid, more fluid and more focused at the same time (Pomodoro, 2013).

The acceptance of social mobility has been quickened with the acceleration and obsolescence of fashion cycles (Burgess, 2012), which have become more recurrent and increasingly rapid. The ephemeral and hypermodern age has ended up creating this collective greed for novelty and stimulation, by a growing differentiation of brands and products, by a rapid turnover of articles and products and by a growing "hyper heterogeneity" of tastes and behaviours. The varieties of personal choice have multiplied and have allowed each individual to make clean, repetitive and flexible choices without any entrenched attachments (Bagozzi et al., 1991).

Fluidity has also affected the fashion industry. It seemed to have embodied discourse of novelty. Brands have adapted to consumer changes and reacted to invest in more services that complement their offerings and have developed more innovative retail formats. Ephemeral stores were the most recent formats responding to postmodern society and they represent "the most emblematic expression of a mobile culture and organization" (Pomodoro, 2013).

3.1.1 Distribution and communication channels and pop-up stores

3.1.1.1 Distribution channels

The beginnings of ephemeral stores were marked by seasonal distribution models (Marks & Sloan, 2003) through physical forms of distribution. Later on, pure players felt the need to come together with the customer base; ephemeral stores have subscribed to this possibility (Clément-Bollée, 2018). Endowed with this fusional characteristic, the ephemeral store is found to complement digital communication (The Storefront, n.d.) and comes even closer to a mode of operation that weaves the physical into the virtual. As the current "postmodern" (InformationAge, 2017) distribution era becomes more and more "hybrid" (PWC, n.d.), consumers find themselves "roaming" freely and pleasantly between brand touchpoints, whether it is a website, a digital platform, a physical or virtual store, or a pop-up store. Delivery following purchases in one channel and receipt in another is at the heart of the customer experience; this is the act of "showrooming" or "webrooming" (Comarch Retail Suite, 2018).

3.1.1.2 Pop-up store communications

In the context of ephemeral stores, communications are given a new meaning that goes beyond the simple transmission of advertising messages. Communications turn into conversational tools between the brand and customers (Martínez Navarro, 2016). The store is at the heart of the conversation (Schwab, 2014), and its experiential aspect (Liza, 2017) involves consumers (Storefront, 2017). Brand/customer conversations grow into customer/customer conversations and lead to creating a "buzz". This online/offline communication and interactions help in making the brand's voice heard.

This will not go unnoticed. Social media networks (Sophelle, Focus Report, 2017) play an important role in building up and sharing messages published by the brand. As consumers live in a society knitted by social networks (Deloitte, 2017), all of these activities will succeed in strengthening brand awareness (The Storefront, n.d.). The status of the ephemeral store is, therefore, "mutated": it represents a "three-dimensional piece of communication" and consequently becomes in itself a means of communication (Schwab, 2014).

3.1.2 Customer-centric and experiential channels

Ephemeral stores meet the expectations of new physical retail experiences with an emotional dimension which is an ideal solution for today's customers (Guingois, 2015) who are asking for fewer products and more experiences. As a response to consumers and their everchanging behaviours, brands are mastering the art of personalizing shopping experiences so that customer visits transform into special moments (Comarch, 2018).

The "downturn generation" appearing post recession (KPMG, 2009) de-envelops a "trained" consumer (PWC, n.d.) who has access and control to information through technology and through which he lives personalized experiences (InsiderTrends, n.d.). Consumers have become, above all, "empowered" internet users (Guingois, 2015; ESCP Europe, 2017) who seek, receive and share information from their "smartphones" (Edwards, 2017).

Millennials (KPMG, 2009; Liza, 2017) are very responsive to ephemeral stores and to the different experiences that revolve around this event. For a frugal "neo-romantic" consumer (PWC, 2017), the important thing is the quest for meaning (ESCP Europe, 2017) and novelty (Liza, 2017). They react against the "consumer society" (Deprez, 2018) as they live by the motto "less is more" (Deloitte, 2017). Today's consumers tend towards using and sharing rather than possessing (TheStorefront, nd); they demand and seek to consume experiences (Influencia, 2017) (Newton, 2017) rather than products. They look for different experiences through different points of contact – physical or virtual. Postmodern consumers are fragmented and belong to microcultures (The Economist. Special issue, 2006): they share their information (Crane, 2018) and their experiences with these cultures via social networks (Harel, 2016). What best describes this consumers is that they are "hybrid" and "instavidual" (KPMG, 2009).

New consumers are more reflective, more alert and aware (KPMG, 2009), more active and constantly looking for ways to learn (Crane, 2018). They do not want to live a shopping experience (Giaimo, 2017) without participating in it. The shopping experience is therefore prone to co-construction (ESCP Europe, 2017) and immersion in experiences (Holmes, 2017; Liza, 2017). This refers to the educational experience based on the active participation of the subject (Martínez Navarro, 2016).

The brand values the collection of personal data from its customers. "Data" helps brands provide consumers with a personalized and exceptional shopping experience (Easiware, 2018). Brands want to address consumers in a different way (Planchard, 2012) by presenting a harmonization between data and distribution channels. A brand's well-thought-out layout can offer consumers with tactile experiences (Steimer, 2017). It is the same idea of "showrooming", allowing consumers to test or try out a product physically following access to information via digital platforms or mobile applications (Edwards, 2017) (Figure 3.1).

3.1.3 Pop-up stores: spaces blurring the barriers between distribution and communications

According to a survey conducted by the leader in experiential marketing, Jack Morton Worldwide (2006), retailers allocate more resources to experiential strategies made up of a set of tangible physical and interactive experiences (Fiore & Kim, 2007) that manifest in one space. In the context of pop-up stores, space is seen as a place of consumption and experience, where brands interact

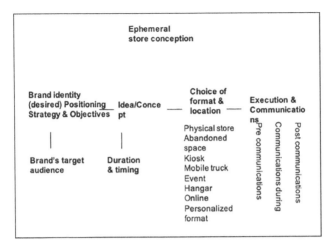

Figure 3.1 Conceiving ephemeral stores.

with consumers. Its function is considered to be a meeting point involving consumers at cognitive and sensory levels. This space is an "interactive and multisensory place" where the brand shares information with the consumer and in which the consumer immerses himself in the experience offered by the brand. This place is as cognitive as it is experiential, as both parties establish a relationship and an emotional exchange. An ephemeral store's space, therefore, becomes a catalyst for an interactive dialogue between a brand and an individual (Russo Spena et al., 2012).

To sum up, ephemeral stores often blur the symbolic order of a physical store. They are not always designed to sell but to immerse users in shared experiences that can include selling products. Brands consider pop-up stores to be places that perfectly allow them to come into direct contact with consumers or the public, to understand user preferences, as well as to co-develop new meanings in their offers. Organizational studies have adopted the spatial turn over the past 15 years, mainly using the space theory of Henri Lefebvre (1991) (Overdiek, 2017).

Yet Lefebvre's theory has been criticized for looking at space from a one-dimensional angle as opposed to conducting a holistic research into the dynamics of planning, practice and integration of space. The reinterpretation of Lefebvre's theory will make it possible to understand spacing simultaneously as a "flow and a thing", and will help to apprehend the ephemeral store as a possible co-actor in the counter-spacing; counter-spacing being defined as "spacing that compensates for other less distinguished spacings" (Overdiek, 2017). Originally rooted in the discipline of marketing, the concept of ephemeral stores has been applied to temporary physical retail environments creating an attractive retail space (Alexander et al., 2018). These stores are designed as "new experiential marketing formats" – formats based on "exclusivity" or formats facilitating marketing communications (Niehm et al., 2007; Pomodoro, 2013; Marciniak & Budnarowska, 2018).

Ephemeral store designs could serve a brand's communications objective, could be conceived to engage customers in immersive experiences or could promote exclusive events or collections.

---

1. Ephemeral stores as experiential marketing formats	Under a promotional framework, ephemeral stores can be designed to offer an exclusive and highly experiential interaction to consumers (Niehm et al., 2007; Lowe et al., 2018).
	The role of pop-up stores as an experiential marketing tool studies the effects on pre-economic success factors such as word of mouth. In this case, there is no evaluation of performance in terms of sales results (Klein et al., 2016).
	Pop-up stores are meant to engage consumers in a series of memorable, hedonistic theatrical experiences. The ephemeral store, as an experiential marketing tool, is seen as an effective "guerrilla marketing" tool. It is unconventional, less expensive and goes beyond traditional printing and distribution media (such as posters, press releases or public transport advertisements). The principle of guerrilla marketing is the development of "buzz" which will then turn into a viral message around the brand, increasing its notoriety (Pomodoro, 2013).
	In the retail context, temporary activations are recognized as an innovative experiential marketing tool that delivers interactive brand experiences and results in increased consumer engagement, driving value for both retailers and consumers (Niehm et al., 2007; Lowe et al., 2018). By providing a new and highly engaging retail experience, temporary activations will prove to be an effective way to test products, generate word of mouth, increase brand awareness and build brand loyalty. These activities have the potential to influence long-term relationships with consumers and aim to generate demand rather than income (Lowe et al., 2018).

(Continued)

Ephemeral store designs could serve a brand's communications objective, could be conceived to engage customers in immersive experiences or could promote exclusive events or collections.

2. Ephemeral stores as formats based on exclusivity	The ephemeral is based on the concept of "here and now" (Alexander et al., 2018). The main reason for consumers to come to these stores is "the anxiety of being left out of the event, of missing out on something unique". Brands create "a surprise effect", a feeling of personal discovery through pop-up stores. And they can achieve this with the short shelf life of the store. That being said, the pop-up store is designed not just as a boutique but as an event. By event, we mean a themed evening, an exhibition or a cocktail party wrapped in an exciting and personalized place (Pomodoro, 2013).
3. Ephemeral stores as marketing communications facilitators	The choice of engaging in promotional applications or proposing a whole marketing mix depends on the size of the company or the brand (whether developed or in development). Facing the changing competitive environment, brands are resorting to several alternative marketing approaches such as expeditionary marketing, guerrilla marketing, disruptive marketing, radical marketing, counterintuitive marketing, buzz, viral or convergence marketing. Guerrilla marketing and viral marketing are key approaches that, at the tactical level, are most applicable to pop-up stores (Marciniak & Budnarowska, 2018; Boustani & Lemoine, 2021).

As for the features characterizing pop-up stores, interconnected factors were found (Taube & Warnaby, 2017): the temporary dimension, the promotional accent and the experiential accent. These characteristics are first presented from a brand's point of view, and secondly, from a consumer's point of view.

The temporal dimension from a brand's point of view: Temporality is an inherent aspect of ephemeral stores; these formats can last a few days and up to a year, their average duration being months. They are often designed in terms of events and their appearances are often subordinate or linked to other events such as a fashion week. The existing literature on experiential marketing and event management highlights the explicit temporality that must be considered when planning pop-up stores. Three process steps have also been identified and linked to the ephemeral store's temporality in general contexts (Taube & Warnaby, 2017):

- **The ephemeral store's pre-phase**: a preparatory phase incorporating strategic decisions such as the store's location, the offer's proposition, the pricing tactics, the atmosphere's design and the promotional and communication methods that need to be planned before the event (often using the brand's social media platforms).
- **The actual contextual experience**: This step consists of perfecting daily decisions and actions that must occur as a result of interactivity or socialization in the pop-up store to generate an experience of the event.
- **The ephemeral store's post-phase**: The brand maintains all communications and exchanges with customers through digital platforms and social media networks. This helps the brand extend the longevity of all experiences that were lived or produced during the ephemeral store's life.

The promotional emphasis: A key goal is that ephemeral stores generate enthusiasm among customers to encourage visits to the store and improve branding. Thus, brands create creative, experiential and promotional environments to avoid customer boredom and generate short-term "buzz". This has several positive implications:

- Given the recent trend of shorter product life cycles and an increase in the number of seasonal collections, pop-up stores offer retailers the ability to respond, with greater flexibility, to changing market needs.
- By promoting new ranges (unique product selections) in a differentiated and unique environment, retailers can create unique experiences that are difficult to replicate.
- Emphasis on the pop-up store as an event can grab media attention and keep the brand relevant in the consumer's minds.

The experiential focus: The pop-up store is defined as a highly experiential environment that aims to communicate the brand or present its offer. If it is properly designed, it will provide visitors with a memorable experience that will ultimately transform their relationship with the brand (Taube & Warnaby, 2017). It has been noted that three elements help create a memorable experience:

- The element of surprise: the element that helps break the routine.
- Entertainment: the more consumers perceive pop-up stores as "happenings", the more they will want to be part of it.
- Fun: to offer a more festive atmosphere, which brings people together and facilitates contacts with the brand representatives of the brand.

The temporary dimension from the consumer's point of view: An ephemeral store's temporary nature can lead to a sense of urgency and a drive to act as customers want to pay a visit before it disappears. Consumer inertia (i.e., in terms of not visiting the pop-up store before it disappears) can lead to a sense of perceived loss as the decision usually cannot be reviewed, and such regret may be higher for more hedonic products.

From the consumer's point of view, social networks are inseparable from pop-up stores, given the "technophile nature" of an ephemeral store and the archetype of consumers who frequent them. In this promotional context, active social media users have a greater awareness and/or knowledge of pop-up store activities and are prone to stimulate word of mouth (Taube & Warnaby, 2017).[1]

This is an experiential dimension of ephemeral stores from the consumer's point of view. These stores create a "surprise effect" through unique products and in-store environments. They attract not only brand advocates but also novices who share many characteristics with the stereotypical ephemeral customer. Ephemeral store atmospheres of pop-up stores are more convivial, spread the offer in a more accessible way and favour spaces that are smaller which facilitate contact with the brand's staff and suggest a "cocooning effect" where customers feel less intimidated. In the context of luxury brands, ephemeral stores generate a bond of seduction between the brand and the customer.

3.2 The new consumer playground

Pop-up stores can be seen as an expression of the impermanent and transient society and the constant search for novelty by consumers. Due to their limited lifetime, they satisfy consumers who constantly look for unique and temporary experiences and who wish to be entertained by interactive performances (Russo Spena et al., 2012).

3.2.1 Innovative consumers looking for something new

Today's consumers increasingly demand memorable and rewarding marketing experiences that dazzle their senses, touch their hearts and stimulate their spirits. They demand products that express their unique personal identity; they want an antidote to the homogenization of choices available on the market (Jones et al., 2017). Besides, they seek novelty (Fowler & Bridges, 2010) and innovative and engaging experiences in all aspects of their lives, including recreational sports, restaurant environments, tourist sites or shopping environments (Kim et al., 2010). Those most interested in ephemeral stores are those defined as experimenters (Pomodoro, 2013), innovators or connoisseurs (market mavens) (Kim et al., 2010).

Consumers have the opportunity to interact with the brand through the various points of contact it offers and ephemeral stores are one of them. Sensitive to changes in consumer behaviour (Chen & Fiore, 2017), the strategy called "pop-up retail" can be designed to promote unique experiences, rich in sensations (Kim et al., 2010), to develop experiences more personal (Jones et al., 2017) or to co-construct or co-create this space. This retail strategy is therefore renewed through pop-up stores by offering novelty to consumers who are not only looking for goods or at least significant entertainment or immediate gratification (Pomodoro, 2013) but also seek uniqueness, discovery, novelty and empathy (Russo Spena et al., 2012).

Ephemeral store experiential marketing approaches[2] lead to positive experiences of consumer interaction with the offer, environment and people present (brand representatives and other customers) (Chen & Fiore, 2017). It is in this interactive, multisensory and authentic environment that a relationship can be built between its different actors (Lowe et al., 2018). It is through social media, word of mouth or during their usual shopping trips to the high-street or commercial outlets that customers discover ephemeral stores (Taube & Warnaby, 2017).

3.2.2 Individual characteristics of consumers interested in pop-up stores

The individual differences between consumers can influence "patronage intentions" towards the choice of stores to frequent. Characteristics that defend retail favouritism include the "impulsiveness, self-regulation, self-confidence and self-congruence" of each individual (Fowler & Bridges, 2010).

The academic literature review identifies women as the "most predisposed" consumers to be interested in ephemeral stores. Studies have shown that age, gender, geographic location and community size influence consumer perceptions of these formats. Other studies have pointed out that "avant-garde or trendy" women eager for innovative and experiential concepts represent the archetypal ephemeral store customers (Taube & Warnaby, 2017). Young, fashion-oriented women who are comfortable with the use of technology are more likely to frequent pop-up stores. These women have a modern and vibrant urban lifestyle. They appreciate the culture of the city and towns and are generally drawn to the most recent and emerging urban trends and experiences (Pomodoro, 2013). Luxury brand ephemeral stores have developed new welcoming, guidance, negotiation and sales techniques aimed at younger consumers (De Lassus & Freire, 2014).[3] Luxury brands invite these consumers to their pop-up stores for an exceptional experience in a context of events and original discovery. The latter prefer short, targeted but repeated exchanges (for confirmation, cancellation, additional information and advice) capable of reassuring them.

Luxury brands traditionally restrict access to their retail stores to create an atmosphere of uniqueness and reverence in an experiential marketing context. This strategy can be perceived today as old fashioned. To overcome this challenge, luxury brands are adopting pop-up stores as an experiential marketing tool aimed at creating brand experiences and increasing word of mouth among existing and new target groups (Klein et al., 2016). These brands are also adopting pop-up stores to "make them perceived as less luxurious" than traditional luxury stores and subsequently lead to less embarrassment among consumers (Lunardo & Mouangue, 2019).

3.2.3 The different types of consumers and their styles of decision-making vis-à-vis ephemeral stores

It turns out that different types of consumers can derive different benefits from their visit to pop-up stores (Chen & Fiore, 2017). Studies in the United States and France (Western markets) have identified hedonic benefit variables (e.g., unique products, exciting experiences), utilitarian (e.g., acquisition of goods), or a combination of both benefits that consumers get after visiting an ephemeral store. However, consumers seek novelty concerning their search of products and look at sources of inspiration for better decision-making during their visit to ephemeral stores.

- Hedonic benefits: Hedonic benefits are non-instrumental and do not seek economic gain. Therefore, the intention is pleasure or enjoyment for itself. Ephemeral stores provide hedonic benefits through experiences (or deals) that promote sensual pleasure.
- Utilitarian benefits: Utilitarian benefits help achieve external goals or objectives, such as economic gain. The utilitarian benefits consumers get from ephemeral stores can come from

several sources. For instance, a consumer's social status can be improved by owning exclusive or rare products, or by being part of a limited number of consumers who have participated in a pop-up marketing event.

• A mix of hedonic and utilitarian advantages: Both advantages can be sought by consumers during their visit to ephemeral stores and can be, for example, a product trial and unique experiences supplemented by a purchase.

The two social actors identified as facilitating ephemeral store marketing communications (Marciniak & Budnarowska, 2018) are "connoisseurs" (also known as avant-garde consumers or market mavens) and "connector" consumers. Other types of social actors also examined in terms of their personality traits are "opinion leaders" and "opinion seekers".

Connoisseurs or avant-garde consumers are those who spend their time collecting intense information about products or services. Connector consumers are those who will have a vast social network of knowledge from various groupings. The desire for social interactions of these consumer types helps with viral transmissions of communicated messages. They are called "proactive co-producers". In terms of personality traits, individuals who use virtual networks to communicate their use of the brand are defined as innovative people and heavy users, and are opinion givers who spend less time using social networking sites. On the other hand, opinion seekers are more sensitive to interpersonal influence. They spend more time using social networking sites.

A recent study carried out in Taiwan (the eastern markets) (Chen & Fiore, 2017) joins some previous results carried out in the Western markets. It showed that hedonic and utilitarian benefit variables related to social gain influence Taiwanese consumer attitudes towards a specific location. The insignificant effect on attitude towards ephemeral stores may have been influenced by the uncertainty associated with the temporary location (the pop-up store is not perceived as a place to buy products). However, these stores' innovative character positively affects the desire for hedonic and utilitarian benefits of the ephemeral store for Taiwanese consumers. Hedonic benefits, such as new experiences offered in the pop-up, are essential elements for Taiwanese innovators to foster a positive attitude towards these stores.

To conclude, this study explored that materialism has a significant effect on the desire for utilitarian benefits. This finding is consistent with studies that have shown that materialistic consumers tend to seek monetary value and improved social status. In the case of ephemeral stores, materialism did not have a significant effect on consumer attitude, and this may be because respondents' attitude was subordinate to the status of brands or events related to the ephemeral store.

It has been argued that the different styles of decision-making between US and UK consumers may be due to cultural or generational differences. A study on millennial decision-making and attitudes towards pop-up stores in the United States found that the difference in results may be due to cross-cultural differences existing in different countries (Shah, 2017).

Millennials are described as the group of people born between the 1980s and 2000s, raised in an era of economic prosperity, informed and adventurous, and behaving in a hedonistic manner with a focus on fun. They are inclined to make spontaneous decisions (Overdiek, 2017). Millennials who want to keep up to date with the latest trends could lean towards choosing new products. This can be explained by the fact that social networks have acculturated this generation to the latest trends conveyed by celebrities and bloggers. In this case, they are considered as "trendy shoppers". It has also been noted that millennials as "recreational shoppers" see shopping as a fun, leisure activity and a shopping trip makes them happy. Previous studies have also found that millennials enjoy shopping and consider it a stress reliever.

Since ephemeral stores are designed to provide an experiential shopping environment, the need for consumer contact would be an important factor when it comes to attitudes towards them. For instance, consumers with a "greater need to touch" showed a positive attitude towards ephemeral stores than consumers with a "lower need to touch". That being said, in an experiential ephemeral store environment, consumers prefer to touch products and live a shopping experience that is rich in emotions. Previous academic research results confirm that consumers' need for contact is positively associated with experiential shopping behaviour and consumers with a "higher need to touch" prefer to buy from a physical store (Overdiek, 2017).

In conclusion, in the context of studying the psychographic characteristics affecting behavioural intentions towards ephemeral stores (Kim et al., 2010), it was revealed that consumers displaying greater innovation and greater enjoyment of shopping were likely to appreciate the positive hedonic ephemeral store aspects, including the excitement and exposure to unique new products. These consumers showed a more positive attitude towards ephemeral stores, as they see these stores as attractive, interesting and enjoyable. This study also looked closely at market mavens to understand that they do not influence the beliefs linked to these stores. While hedonic and utilitarian beliefs were linked to attitude towards pop-up stores, the study found that beliefs about hedonic aspects (more than utilitarian aspects) seemed to be the draw for consumers. So, an individual's attitude towards ephemeral stores is positively associated with recommending, trying and buying products.

In an increasingly globalized retail market, socioeconomic and demographic changes are altering consumer behaviour, purchasing habits and retail sales models. These behaviours are also influenced by the development and acceleration of new technologies (Lowe et al., 2018). While there are examples of physical stores in decline due to increased competition from e-commerce and new digital retail logic, there are also examples of new retail formats and adjustments in retail concepts that reinforce the role of the physical store (Hagberg et al., 2016). One of the strategies retailers employ to cope with changes in consumer behaviour and overcome the threats of e-commerce is the temporary activation of retail (Lowe et al., 2018).

Physical stores are impacting and are being impacted by the retail digitalization. Many online retailers are introducing new concepts of physical temporary stores to complement their online businesses. Online stores, for example, provide a longer shelf life of the brand's offer, which is very limited in an ephemeral store (Jones et al., 2017). Also, ephemeral stores are seen as a key part of the omnichannel concept that is becoming more and more common in the retail landscape. The ephemeral store is now part of an omnichannel retail marketing strategy, with brand communication and improved experience being the dominant themes (Hagberg et al., 2016; Alexander et al., 2018). Digital devices are also increasingly populating physical stores and are supplied by retailers or brought in by consumers and increasingly connected. So, rather than separating digitalization from retail, we are now seeing initiatives for the integration of digital and physical retail logic (Hagberg et al., 2016).

While the phenomenon of pop-up stores has been reported in many parts of the world, different attestations have been made for the origins of these stores. It has been suggested that pop-up stores appeared in the United States and European cities around 2003 (Burgess, 2012; Pomodoro, 2013; Edward Spragg, 2017). Other sources claim that pop-up stores started in London in 1999 with Levi's and Swatch (De Lassus, 2012). However, the origins of pop-up stores are actually linked to the opening of a branded fashion boutique in Tokyo by an American company, Vacant, in 1999 (Edward Spragg, 2017). It was, therefore, explained that the concept of pop-up stores creates a stir, arouses media interest, and arouses consumer curiosity. This new store formula is developing a lot not only in the United States, Asia and the Gulf regions (Picot-Coupey, 2012) but also more recently in Europe with, for example, the Nutella chalet, installed in Paris during the winter of 2011 (De Lassus, 2012). Despite their ephemeral natures, these formats are now made to subsist among a brand's distribution and/or communication channels (Tansel, 2017) and are instead developed and presented through physical formats.

Notes

1 Social media networks are adopted by brands during the three key phases of an ephemeral store (pre, during and post): during the pre–pop-up phase, brands can communicate their messages or information using messages (SMS), blogs or through social networks. One of the most widely used communication strategies is the dissemination of precise information to "opinion leaders" who will then relay the information received within their networks. At the post–pop-up stage, social networks can be used to create a "chain of communication that could extend across an entire community" (Taube & Warnaby, 2017) that can be seen as more credible than traditional advertising communications.

2 Experiential marketing focuses on creating personal, memorable and engaging experiences that enhance brand awareness and appreciation. Schmitt (1999) proposed five types of experiential marketing approaches: sense (sight, sound, touch, taste and smell), sensation (emotional arousal), reflection (cognitive engagement), the act (physical behaviours, lifestyles and interactions), and relating (being part of a social context). For example, memorable ephemeral retail experiences come from direct observation and/or participation (meaning), highly innovative or limited-edition products (think or feel), elaborate and/or unconventional store structures (e.g., a store in the shape of a giant shoebox), unique lifestyle events (acting) and personal interactions with knowledgeable brand representatives and passionate customers (related) (Chen & Fiore, 2017).

3 We can describe these consumers as "digital natives". They are solicited by brands through NTIs, "new technological instruments" such as blogs, forums or social networks.

References

Alexander, B., Nobbs, K. & Varley, R., 2018. The growing permanence of pop-up outlets within the international location strategies of fashion retailers. *International Journal of Retail & Distribution Management*, 46(5), pp. 487–506.

Badot, O., Lemoine, J.-F. & Ochs, A., 2018. *Distribution 4.0.* 1st ed. s.l.: Pearson.

Bagozzi, R. Y., Yi, Y. & Philips, L. W., 1991. Assessing validity construct in organizational research. *Administrative Science Quarterly*, 36, pp. 421–458.

Bauman, Z. (2000), Liquid Modernity, Polity Press, Cambridge.

Boustani, G. & Lemoine, J-F., 2021. « An ephemeral point of sale's atmospheric dimensions ». 20th International Congress Marketing Trends. January 14–16, 2021, Venice. Italy.

Burgess, B., 2012. Pop-up retailing: The design, implementation, and five-year evolution of an experiential learning project. *Journal of Marketing Education*, 34(3), pp. 284–296.

Chen, W.-C. & Fiore, A. M., 2017. Factors affecting Taiwanese consumers' responses toward pop-up retail. *Asia Pacific Journal of Marketing and Logistics*, 29(2), pp. 370–392.

Clément-Bollée, B., 2018. *What's in store for the future of retail ? Physical storefronts with digital touchpoints.* [Online] Available at: http://blog. thestorefront.com/whats-in-store-for-the-future-of-retail-physical-storefronts-with-digital-touchpoints/ [Accessed 16 04 2018].

Comarch, 2018. *Expérience client et fidélisation - les grandes tendances à venir en 2018.* [Online] Available at: www.comarch.fr [Accessed 19 02 2018].

Comarch Retail Suite, 2018. *Le retail hybrid.* [Online] Available at: www. comarch.fr [Accessed 12 04 2018].

Crane, A., 2018. *Brandless' 'pop-up with purpose' focuses on community over product.* [Online] Available at: https://mail.google.com/mail/u/0/#inbox/ 163f32d31ce59823 [Accessed 07 08 2018].

De Lassus, C., 2012. Les pop-up stores de luxe : entre lieu mythique et endroit éphémère, une analyse sémiotique. *Colloque Etienne Thil*, Lille, France.

De Lassus, C. & Freire, A., 2014. Access to the luxury brand myth in pop-up stores: A netnographic and semiotic analysis. *Journal of Retailing and Customer Services*, 21, pp. 61–68.

Deloitte, 2017. *Global powers of retailing 2017. The art and science of customers.* [Online] Available at: https://www.google.fr/search?q=the+art+and+ science+of+retail+reinvention&oq=the+art+and+science+of+retail+ reinvention+&aqs=chrome.69i57.8243j0j4&sourceid= chrome&ie=UTF-8 [Accessed 06 12 2017].

Deprez, L., 2018. *Dada s'installe en pop-up au printemps.* [Online] Available at: FashionNetwork.com [Accessed 06 02 2018].

Easiware, 2018. *La data: incontournable pour une expérience client de choc.* [Online] Available at: www.easiware.com [Accessed 11 05 2018].

Edwards, J., 2017. *The most astonishing and predictable trend in economics just got more astonishing and predictable.* [Online] Available at: http:// www.businessinsider.fr/uk/online-share-of-retail-economics-2017-12/ [Accessed 05 01 2018].

Edward Spragg, J., 2017. Articulating the fashion product life-cycle. *Journal of Fashion Marketing and Management: An International Journal*, 21(4), pp. 499–511.

ESCP Europe, 2017. *La co-construction de l'expérience.* [Online] Available at: http://www.escpeurope.eu/nc/media-news/news-newsletter/news-single/article/la-co-construction-de-lexperience-shopping-a-lere-de-leconomie-collaborative-et-numerique/ [Accessed 11 08 2017].

Fiore, A. M. & Kim, J., 2007. An integrative framework capturing experiential and utilitarian shopping experience. *International Journal of Retail and Distribution Management*, 35(6), pp. 421–442.

Fowler, K. & Bridges, E., 2010. Consumer innovativeness: Impact on expectations, perceptions, and choice among retail formats. *Journal of Retailing and Consumer Services*, 17, pp. 492–500.

Giaimo, A., 2017. *Real estate days.* [Online] Available at: https://media10.simplex.tv/content/73/4448/91335/ [Accessed 11 08 2018].

Guingois, S., 2015. *Pop-up store: Le nouveau format vedette du retail.* [Online] Available at: www.IFLS.net [Accessed 15 04 2018].

Hagberg, J., Sundstrom, M. & Egels-Zandén, N., 2016. The digitalization of retailing: An exploratory framework. *International Journal of Retail & Distribution Management*, 44(7), pp. 694–712.

Harel, C., 2016. *Magnum ouvre un bar éphémère au Carrefour de Villiers-en-Bière.* [Online] Available at: https://www.lsa-conso.fr/magnum-ouvre-un-bar-ephemere-au-carrefour-de-villiers-en-biere,239940 [Accessed 12 02 2018].

Holmes, N., 2017. *Pop-ups: An essential part of the modern retail strategy.* [Online] Available at: http://www.jllrealviews.com/industries/pop-ups-an-essential-part-of-the-modern-retail-strategy/ [Accessed 08 11 2017].

Influencia, 2017. *Influencia.* [Online] Available at: http://www.influencia.net/fr/actualites/art-culture,luxe,pop-up-store-levier-experientiel-luxe,7802.html [Accessed 13 11 2017].

InformationAge, 2017. *The dawn of post modern retailing.* [Online] Available at: http://www.information-age.com/top-5-best-ways-promote-online-shopping-business-123462340/ [Accessed 07 01 2018].

InsiderTrends, n.d. *Top 50 innovations in retail.* [Online] Available at: www.insidertrends.com [Accessed 07 01 2018].

Jack Morton Worldwide, (2006). Jack Morton Worldwide releases experiential marketing study. [Online] Available at: https://www.exhibitoronline.com/news/article.asp?ID=4198 [Accessed 04 06 2020].

Jones, P., Comfort, D. & Hillier, D., 2017. A commentary on pop up shops in the UK. *Property Management*, 35(5), pp. 545–553.

Kim, H., Fiore, A., Niehm, L. & Jeong, M., 2010. Psychographic characteristics affecting behavioral intentions towards pop-up retail. *International Journal of Retail & Distribution Management*, 38(2), pp. 133–154.

Klein, J. F., Falk, T., Esch, F.-R. & Gloukhovtsev, A., 2016. Linking pop-up brand stores to brand experience and word of mouth: The case of luxury retail. *Journal of Business Research*, 69(12), pp. 5761–5767.

KPMG, 2009. *The evolution of retailing. Reinventing the customer experience.* [Online] Available at: us.kpmg.com [Accessed 11 01 2018].

Lipovetsky, G. (2004), *Les Temps Hypermodernes*, Editions Grasset, Paris.

Liza, 2017. *Le journal du Luxe.* [Online] Available at: https://journalduluxe. fr/pop-up-stores-strategie-marques/ [Accessed 13 11 2017].

Lowe, J., Maggioni, I. & Sands, S., 2018. Critical success factors of temporary retail activations: A multi-actor perspective. *Journal of Retailing and Consumer Services*, 40, pp. 175–185.

Lunardo, R. & Mouangue, E., 2019. Getting over discomfort in luxury brand stores: How pop-up stores affect perceptions of luxury, embarrassment, and store evaluations. *Journal of Retailing and Consumer Services*, pp. 77–85.

Marciniak, R. & Budnarowska, C., 2018. *Exploration of pop-up retail: The department store perspective.* Belgium, 4th International colloquium on design, branding and marketing (ICDBM).

Marks, J. & Sloan, C., 2003. Hit-and-run retailing. *Home Textiles Today*, 01 12.

Martínez Navarro, G., 2016. *El retail experiencial: un nuevo enfoque en la comunicación de marca.* Madrid-España: Universidad Complutense de Madrid-España.

Miotto, A. P. & Gomes Parente, J., 2015. Retail evolution model in emerging markets: Apparel store formats in Brazil. *International Journal of Retail & Distribution Management,* 43(3), pp. 242–260.

Newton, A., 2017. *6 reasons why pop-up stores are excelling.* [Online] Available at: https://retailnext.net/en/blog/6-reasons-why-pop-up-stores-are-excelling/[Accessed 11 01 2018].

Niehm, L. S., Ann Marie, F., Jeong, M. & Kim, H.-J., 2007. Pop-up retail's acceptability as an innovative business strategy and enhancer of the consumer shopping experience. *Journal of Shopping Center Research*, 13(7), pp. 1–30.

Overdiek, A., 2017. Fashionable interventions: The pop-up store as differential space. *Organizational Aesthetics*, 6(1), pp. 116–134.

Pantano, E. & Dennis, C., 2017. Exploring the origin of retail stores in Europe: Evidence from southern Italy from the 6th century BCE to the 3d century BCE. *Journal of Retailing and Customer Services*, 39, pp. 243–249.

Picot-Coupey, K., 2012. Pop-up stores and the international development of retail networks. *International marketing trends conference*, Venice, Italy.

Picot-Coupey, K., 2013. Les voies d'avenir du magasin physique à l'heure du commerce connecté. *Gestion*, 38(2), pp. 51–61.

Planchard, C., 2012. *« Les boutiques éphémères », un concept bien parti pour durer.* [Online] Available at: http://www.20minutes.fr/economie/945305-20120601-les-boutiques-ephemeres-concept-bien-parti-durer [Accessed 14 11 2017].

Pomodoro, S., 2013. Temporary retail in fashion system: An explorative study. *Journal of Fashion Marketing and Management: An international Journal*, 17(3), pp. 341–352.

PWC, 2017. *2017 Retail and industry trends, showrooms, retail experience and compelling economics.* [Online] Available at: www.strategyand.pwc. com [Accessed 11 01 2018].

PWC, n.d. *Retailing 2020: Winning a polarized world.* [Online] Available at: www.pwc/us/retailandconsumer [Accessed 05 01 2018].

Russo Spena, T., Caridà, A., Colurcio, M. & Melia, M., 2012. Store experience and co-creation: The case of temporary shop. *International Journal of Retail & Distribution Management*, 40(1), pp. 21–40.

Schmitt, B., 1999. Experiential marketing. *Journal of Marketing Management*, 15, pp. 53–67.

Schwab, P.-N., 2014. *Pop-up stores: ce qu'ils révèlent sur l'avenir du commerce de détail.* [Online] Available at: http://www.intotheminds.com/blog/pop-up-stores-ce-quils-revelent-lavenir-du-commerce-detail/ [Accessed 16 04 2018].

Shah, A., 2017. Exploring millennials' decision-making styles and their attitudes towards pop-up stores. *ProQuest LLC*, p. 110.

Sophelle, Focus Report, 2017. *Boundaryless.* [Online] Available at: https://www.sophelle.com/focus-report-download-form/ [Accessed 17 11 2017].

Steimer, S., 2017. *The magic of pop-u shop marketing.* [Online] Available at: https://www.ama.org/publications/MarketingNews/Pages/magic-of-pop-up-shop-marketing.aspx [Accessed 11 02 2018].

Storefront, 2017. *How Brit + Co created a pop-up community.* [Online] Available at: http://blog.thestorefront.com/fr/how-brit-co-created-a-pop-up-community/ [Accessed 18 02 2018].

Tansel, U., 2017. Licensors and Retailers Increasingly Experiment with the "Pop-up" Store Model in Licensing. *Euromonitor International*, pp. 1–2.

Taube, J. & Warnaby, G., 2017. How brand interaction in pop-up shops influences consumers' perceptions of luxury fashion retailers. *Journal of Fashion Marketing and Management: An International Journal*, 21(3), pp. 385–399.

The Storefront, n.d. *Future of retail desires temporary experiences.* [Online] Available at: http://blog.thestorefront.com/future-of-retail-desires-temporary-experiences/ [Accessed 11 09 2017].

4 Understanding the future by looking at the past

To examine the evolution and change in retailing, a distinction needs to be made between the "macro" and "micro" scale relating to changes in the retail environment. The theory of evolution appeals to notions of change and development, which have been explained by phenomena of regularity or cyclicity. It is important to examine different stages of evolution to understand how retail has become what it is today.

4.1 Retail life cycles and retail formats

The starting point for macro-scale analysis is to observe the space in which retailing operates and which offers opportunities or constraints for further developments; this space is called "the design space". It is made up of six distinct categories which together affect the development of retail. The first category concerns the size of the aggregate population and its spatial distribution over a given region, which will determine the overall need for goods in this area. The second category concerns the structure of needs, which affects and is affected by family size and income allocation. Then, the third category considers the total income of the region and the distribution of this income across the population. The fourth category is technology, which has a major impact on both consumers and retailers. The fifth category is government regulation, which can constrain or encourage both supply and demand of the trading process. The last category that has been added to the list is the socio-cultural facet that helps determine whether retailers or consumers will be able to "see" a particular part of the retail space (which is socially visible or invisible) that is considered a legitimate environment to sell among many other environments (Keri, 1998).

Authors have identified a set of specific environmental factors that appear to be related to the development of retail trade and, further, established how retail was affected. In turn, they highlighted six influential variables. The first category concerns the degree of specialization of products in retail stores, the aggressiveness of the sales methods of manufacturers and wholesalers or, conversely, consumers' preference for neighbourhood stores. This first category relates to direct per capita income, population density and population urbanization. The second category explains the extent of self-service use which is directly related to population density. The third category concerns literacy on one hand, and newspaper and communication circulation and consumers' preference for daily purchases in small quantities on the other hand. As for the fourth category, it is concerned with the application of sophisticated margin policies (also concerning literacy). The fifth category looks at the extent of use of retail advertising and is a direct function of literacy and an inverse function of consumers' preference for daily purchases in small quantities. The last category explains whether the extent of the use of loss leaders (loss leaders) is a direct function of the literacy and aggressiveness of manufacturer and wholesaler sales methods, or a function of consumer preference for buying on credit (Wadinambiaratchi & Girvan, 1972).

Environmental models highlight the influence of the socio-economic environment on business structures. According to these approaches, it is the changes in economic and social, demographic, cultural, regulatory or even technological conditions that are at the origin of the institutional changes affecting commerce. Business formats appear and develop in direct reaction to environmental circumstances and environmental conditions. It is therefore existing environmental conditions that best explain the emergence of such and such a store format, or such a sales formula (Gallouj & Gallouj, 2009). Change is a response to prevailing environmental factors and can be linear or cyclical. Although the academic literature adopts each type of change separately, it has been found that these views are not fundamentally irreconcilable. Innovations in retail are critical to the success of retailers. These are judged to be sensitive to the characteristics of markets, namely mature, emerging and less developed markets. It has also been explained how some retailers have succeeded in turning difficult market conditions into retail opportunities through innovation (Shankar & Yadav, 2011).

The two points of view may not be fundamentally irreconcilable. After all, if a vehicle has to move forward... it must be carried on wheels which turn monotonously and round.

(Brown, 1990)

As Van de Ven and Poole (1995, p. 515) comment, alongside teleology, the life cycle is perhaps the most common explanation for development in managerial literature.

(Lowson, 2005)

Previous studies have led to a growing awareness of marketing metaphors, of which the wheel is a particularly compelling example. Not only does it include connotations of the Greco-Roman wheel of fortune, but it also manages, remarkably, to integrate the notions of recurrence (cycle) and progression (arrow) (Brown, 1990). In management science, several hypotheses have been suggested regarding retail trade development patterns.

There are two distinct types of conceptualization of the evolutionary models of food retail systems. First, the "stage"-type assumptions which focus on one-way development trends where changes and retail institutions are said to consist of a series of development stages ranging from a simple to a more complex version of the institution. Then, there are the "cycle" assumptions about patterns that are likely to repeat over time. Cycle assumptions have been described as one of the most important developments in (food) retail (Erdener & Cavusgil, 1982).

Professor McNair proposed a major hypothesis concerning the retail development model. It explains that new types of retailers generally enter the market as operators of low status and who sell at low prices and low margins. Gradually, they acquire more sophisticated establishments and facilities (which McNair describes as gentrification (Chanut & Paché, 2013)), with both increased investments and higher operating costs. Finally, they improve their status and sell at a high price; at this stage, they become vulnerable to new retail types which, in turn, follow the same pattern (Hollander, 1996) (Wadinambiaratchi & Girvan, 1972).

Available retail formats meet consumer needs and continue to evolve as communications technology advances (Bradley & LaFleur, 2016). More sophisticated and "high-end" sales formats are the result of the development of the retail wheel. This movement manifests itself in the improvement of commercial space images and the improvement of their services. Industrial spaces that are transformed into "parks", for example, are becoming more and more sophisticated. They are viewed from the outset as clustered developments and, in response to social trends, sometimes include recreational uses (Gibbs, 1987).

As modern retail institutions and practices evolve towards greater global acceptance, the opportunities in developing countries are especially promising; yet, small retailers still dominate in many of these countries (Evans, 2011). These retailers may not be able to adapt to a cyclical pattern by going through all of these stages. However, they will manage their development organically (Lowson, 2005). This explanation is known as the "wheel of retailing".

Six tentative explanations for several environmental factors causing configuration changes at the "wheel" have been presented (Hollander, 1960). A first explanation concerns the retail personality. New types of retail establishments are often created by very aggressive and cost-conscious entrepreneurs who count every penny and are not interested in "unprofitable frills". A second explanation is "straying". It was explained that retail reviews encourage retailers to do unnecessary "modernization" and install overly elaborate equipment. A third explanation is that of "imperfect competition". Although retail is often cited as the only type of business that comes close to Adam Smith's concept of perfect competition, some economists have argued that retail is a good example of imperfect competition. Then, a fourth explanation is that of the "excess capacity" which unfolds over the entries of retailers in any branch of commerce. "Illusion" is the fifth explanation. This shows that cross-merchandising trends can create illusory "wheel" trends as they tend to show an average increase in the brand's margin. The last explanation relates to "secular trends" in the market. Raising the standard of living in a country will create profitable opportunities for traders.

Many management researchers have adopted the organic growth metaphor as a heuristic device to explain the development of an organizational entity from its initiation to its completion. It has been argued that social and economic environments help and dictate the development of both retail and retail institutions. Hollander, therefore, suggests that the distribution "wheel" can only turn if the environment is favourable for the successful introduction of an innovation. Cundiff adds that the "retail wheel" theory can only be applied in the most developed economies (Wadinambiaratchi & Girvan, 1972) (Ingene, 2014). At this point, the concept of a life cycle requires some exploration (Lowson, 2005).

The concept of cyclicality also applies to products and consumption (Lemaitre & De Barnier, 2015) (Tibben-Lembke, 2002). After the product is introduced, sales start to slowly increase, until a critical mass of consumer awareness is achieved, and then sales increase rapidly. Eventually, the rapid growth cools and the product enters a period of sustained slow growth or stable sales. Eventually, sales will decline, slowly at first, then perhaps faster. Once the sales fall below a certain threshold (which may be different for each business), the product will eventually be discontinued and sales will drop to zero. Four phases, therefore, characterize a product's life cycle: introduction, development, maturity and decline (or regression) (Tibben-Lembke, 2002; Edward Spragg, 2017). As for the consumption cycle, it breaks down into three phases: acquisition, consumption and dispossession (Lemaitre & De Barnier, 2015).

The study of the dynamics of distribution formulas dates back to the work of Alderson (1957) and Bucklin (1960) (Rieunier & Volle, 2002). Environmental theories argue that the retail system's structure reflects changes in the surrounding market's economic, demographic, social, cultural and technological conditions (Keri, 1998). Although these theories examine the retail environment, they all give the consumer a prominent role in being able to explain the commercial dynamics (Chanut & Paché, 2013; Miotto & Gomes Parente, 2015). Brown's (1987) review was the most widely accepted on the evolution of retail trade. She distils the literature into three main approaches to understanding the transformation process: cyclical, conflictual and environmental (McArthur et al., 2016).

The first attempts at studies of the dynamics of distribution forms were essentially based on an economic approach. The wheel of distribution theory has developed and various theories, such as the theory of the life cycle or the accordion, have come to complete the set (Rieunier & Volle, 2002). The reference to the life cycle refers to the biological life cycle by analogy. It is commonly represented by a so-called S-curve. The cycle is divided into phases from birth, growth, maturity and until death (Vandaele, 1986; Rao, 2009).

The retail environment is constantly changing and appears to continue to evolve as it contracts and expands; during this shift, many forms of retail will evolve, change, appear or disappear. Since retailing is a contextual discipline, its characteristics vary across regions depending on local economic, social and institutional conditions (Miotto & Gomes Parente, 2015). The customer is a vital part of this equation as they have the power to influence the retailer's proposals and strategic decisions. The study of retail formats

(Antéblian & Filser, 2008) is a constant in distribution research. Sales "format" refers to all operating and merchandising tactics and practices used by the retail business to distinguish and differentiate itself from other competitive retail formats. Competitive advantages are realized by creating a retail format tailored to the specific needs of a carefully determined segment of the total market (Alexander, 2008). So, the term "format" is frequently used in a simple way to identify the type of retail store that interests him.

To better visualize and understand variations in "sales formats", they can be viewed as "combinations of technologies" and retail as the "bundling of these technologies" in the manner deemed "most appropriate for the market". In a more detailed examination of the nature of the format, it consists of two parts: the supply (external) and the know-how (internal) (Alexander, 2008). Any retail format's performance depends on several other parameters such as location, space allocated, the composition of merchandise, visibility, level of sales employees and service (Malhotra, 2007).

Determining a store's format reflects the defined retail strategy. Retail sales strategies and store formats are therefore closely linked (Miotto & Gomes Parente, 2015). A retail format refers to the structures of sequencing and organizing selected retail activities into cohesive processes that respond to the customer experience. Specifically, the format represents a combination of particular levels of each element of the retail mix elements, such as product assortment, pricing strategy, location or customer interface. In any product category, several formats are generally feasible and different customers choose the format (s) that best meet their needs (Sorescu et al., 2011). It is possible to meet definitions referring to "formats" as being "points of sale" (Botschen & Wegerer, 2017) in which actions are carried out which make it possible to prepare a ticket and/or a sales invoice, to control inventories and business operations (Felipe, n.d.). It is finally recognized that in addition to transactions, the retail point of sale also induces certain relational practices (Senkel, 2002).

Several sales formats have been the result of each stage of the retail disruption. Retailers increasingly depend on the success of new offline and online retail formats and their innovations in support and organization at the strategic and operational levels to secure competitive advantages and drive future growth (Alexander, 2008) (Botschen & Wegerer, 2017). Among the formats that are more attractive to consumers and meet their preferences (Rousey & Morganosky, 1996) are outdoor centres, regional centres, "pull destinations" (Reynolds et al., 2007) or pop-up stores (Marciniak & Budnarowska, 2018) (De Lassus, 2012); as for traditional shopping centres or downtown districts, they are in a difficult situation (Niehm et al., 2007).

4.2 The evolution and revolution of retail

4.2.1 The evolution and disruption of retail

> [...] At this stage, the municipal policy is overthrown and replaced by an entirely different policy; citizens must trade their products in the market by buying and selling. The new arrangement, like the first, distributes among the citizens the different goods that they each produce. But now many institutions associated with commerce and the market are also introduced: traders and sailors, services and retail, even fiat currency and wage labour. For the modern eye, a real revolution has been instituted. Plato's interlocutors, on the other hand, are unfazed, frankly sketching out the reasoning and taking the changes smoothly.
>
> (Doubman, 1935)

Commerce and shopping districts date back to "the agora of ancient Greece". The bazaars of Jerusalem and Istanbul have been providing a covered market shopping experience for 2,000 years. In the Middle Ages, the sale of goods was done beyond the city walls to avoid taxes; a tax, on the other hand, should be paid to the feudal authority. In England, the town of Chester has been famous for centuries for its interconnected second-floor shops that stretch out in blocks across the city centre. Although modern retailing dates back to the beginning of the Industrial Revolution, significant retail activity continued over a much longer period. Modern retail practices are evolutionary, not revolutionary (Evans, 2011).

Historical evidence from Great Britain (Novak, 2010) describes important moments in the development of trade in the country. We return to a time when farmers took advantage of the favourable growing conditions the region offered, clearing and cultivating the fertile land and erecting houses and barns. Grid streets were formed comprising a series of uniform blocks, each divided into ten lots of equal size. The retail sector had already started with the first store in one of the settlements. Its location occupies the main street (later becoming a shopping street in the city); this trade was joined by two taverns. The earliest links with areas beyond the village were primitive at best. From 1827, it took four days to cover a period of 400 km between two villages via London; thus, it took two days in either direction to reach a port from where goods could be shipped by sea – the ideal form of transportation at the time. Due to the small isolated market, products offered by retailers in London were a little varied. Besides, the isolation meant that most consumers were unaware of the variety of products available elsewhere.

Due to poor transport links, local retailers' product supply was severely limited. In addition to limiting product selection, smaller markets have motivated retailers to diversify their operations to make ends meet. Some added financial services such as real estate and loans while others were involved in the production process. For some, this diversification was successful, while for others, the benefits were still elusive. The City of London's industrial sector developed soon after the arrival of the first inhabitants, ensuring the economic growth of the developing colony. Early industries were important to the retail sector in two general ways: first, producers manufacturing provided local outlets for merchandise, and second, industries provided an economic base; those who worked in the industry spent their wages securing goods at local retailers.

At the time of its incorporation as a city, London had a well-established and complex retail system. Many other locals living in the surrounding countryside and neighbouring towns travelled to London to frequent its shops, which helped its market flourish. This market growth has allowed more stores to offer a greater variety of products. The arrival of the railway in December 1853 was of great importance to the continued development of London. Trains have made travel faster and more comfortable, and moved large quantities of goods quickly, carefully and inexpensively. Local retailers could secure more goods at a lower cost of transportation which led to a wider product selection. They could now respond more quickly to customer demands, placing orders with wholesalers in the East that would be filled quickly (Novak, 2010). As in Britain, transport has made a significant contribution to the development of trade, exchanges and the development of the offer in other countries.

Retailing has undergone significant changes in five main areas since the arrival of department stores around the 1800s: formats, technologies, forms of ownership, types of customers and geography (McArthur et al., 2016). The growth of the economy, together with the evolution of public transport and new forms of mass production, also contributed to the expansion of stores and businesses in the late 19th and early 20th centuries (Woodruffe-Burton, 2001).

For the first time, consumers (especially women) have been able to take advantage, thanks to the development of the department store, of a public space specially designed for activities that meet their functional, social and ambitious needs. Many department stores, described as "cathedrals of consumption", became fantastic purpose-built luxury venues that offered a range of entertainment (Woodruffe-Burton, 2001). These large stores tended to decrease the performance of small and specialized retailers, a classic feature of disruption in the retail industry (Slywotzky et al., 2000) (Table 4.1).

After the 1930s, the pace of retail development accelerated; changes occurred faster, were more random and were more interdependent (McNair & May, 1978). In Western countries, the most visible change has been the transition of stores through a sequence of different formats. In rough chronological order of their development, the major retail formats have been small general stores, department stores, chain stores, supermarkets, discount department stores, franchises, "category killers" and online stores (McArthur et al., 2016).

As consumers became dependent on the automobile, suburban retail outlets began to be clustered and located to meet the new behaviours of motorized consumers. Suburban stores replaced the neighbourhood stores that had been located for the convenience of pedestrians. Thus, the automobile age led to another institutional change, the suburban shopping centre (McNair & May, 1978).

After World War II, many shopping centres developed in the suburbs. Equally important is the growing demand from an increasingly affluent, socially and geographically mobile urban population

Table 4.1 The first department stores

The first department stores in the world (Chevrel, 2012)
1854 Paris, France Le Bon Marché (Mr Aristide Boucicaut)
1860 Paris, France The Bazar of the "Hôtel de Ville"
1865 Paris, France Le Printemps & La Samaritaine
1896 Paris, France The Galeries Lafayette
1890 London, England Harrods & Whiteley
1907 Chicago, United States Marshall Field's
1909 London, England Selfridges (Mr Harry Gordon Selfridge)
1930 Berlin, Germany Karstadt

(Woodruffe-Burton, 2001). Thanks to this development, suburban housing and automobiles became interdependent. In relatively few years, sales at large self-service stores (and discount stores) have more than matched those of conventional department stores. As it happened, the store with few price varieties all but disappeared. As these changes were occurring in the general merchandise sector, food supermarkets grew larger by expanding not only their food lines but also a lot of non-food items such as paper goods, toiletries, basic-wear and household items (McNair & May, 1978).

During the 1960s, furniture warehouses and catalogue showrooms as well as activities of specialized mail order saw significant growth. These companies specialized in fashion and home furnishings and sought to serve consumers seeking fashion, prestige and quality, and able to pay the price offered. Finally, speciality store chains have appeared in the leisure market (McNair & May, 1978). Commerce and distribution grow, improve or change shape depending on the prevailing market conditions. In almost all economic systems, the retail distribution of goods and services is a vital link in the distribution channel, from production to consumption. Retail activity volumes are much larger in developed countries than in developing countries; the more economically developed a company is, the more important and complex the functions of retail distribution. In less developed economies, some form of local exchange has been recorded (Paddison et al., 1990).

It was once predicted that shopping would become "store-less" in the 1970s (Watson et al., 2002). For the majority of brands, shopping is not yet virtual. However, with the recent emergence and growth of e-merchants and the trend in retailing of offering online services, it is clear that not only is the technology available but there is a growing acceptance from customers. Almost inevitably, the trend towards electronic shopping will increase and affect, but not erase, the expansion of physical retail. Even though shoppers have the technology and expertise to shop online, shopping has become a leisure experience that many current consumers will want to attend. Under such circumstances, it would appear that retail will continue to expand, at least in the short to medium term.

The internet caused the fourth disruption (Cundiff, 1965; Slywotzky et al., 2000), and its emergence has fundamentally altered the retail landscape as the three previous disruptions. Technological breakthroughs add to the list of variables influencing the retail industry. Individuals have become more informed than ever and, using technological tools, could even produce the offer themselves (prosumers) (Lipkin, 2016).

Retail developed and changed shape over the years. The evolutions to remember are (McNair & May, 1978), first of all, the passage from the specialization to the heterogeneity of products. Then, there has been a rise in the indirect but significant relationships between changes in retailing and economic, technological, demographic and social changes. Looking closely at the last 30 or 40 years, indications of impending changes in retail establishments were pointed out; changes that herald a major turning point in the distribution wheel. It is added that there has been an acceleration of socio-economic change and an apparent shortening of various types of retail business life cycles and the rise of mass distribution. The consumer becomes a key element in influencing change in retailing and technology directly affects change in retailing.

The points of sale bear witness to the constant changes brought about by the continuous technological progresses. These innovations can be seen as catalysts for change that have radically altered the retail landscape, driven by the need to provide new entertainment experiences to consumers (Pantano & Dennis, 2017). The future role of the physical store is unclear, and it could end up being determined by product category and customer segment. The traditional store could change its role into a "hub", the focal point that would integrate all sales channels. It is possible to use the store as a place to provide a personal experience that will attract customers, regardless of the channel used (Piotrowicz & Cuthbertson, 2014). Now retailers are best described as orchestrators or drivers of two-way platforms that serve as ecosystems in which value is created and delivered to customers and, subsequently, appropriated by the retailer and its business partners. Retail is no longer seen as spaces (physical or virtual) for staging customer experiences; it requires business models that go beyond the traditional functions of supplying, storing and moving products (Sorescu et al., 2011).

As brands are faced with fierce competition in today's retail environment on one hand and facing escalating customer expectations on the other hand, they are looking at ways to innovate their businesses to build a sustainable competitive advantage. (Sorescu et al., 2011). Retailers are implementing innovations of strategic, operational and relational nature (Sansone & Colamatteo, 2017). The strategic dimension refers to innovations that affect the store's image perceived by consumers, thanks to the communication activities implemented by the company. The second level is the operational dimension that refers to more traditional methods of value creation using the marketing mix levers: assortment, communication, sales environment and services, all of which are important elements of strengthening the commercial offer. As for the third level, relational, it includes innovative actions involving non-traditional areas of value creation but refers to the introduction of new instruments affecting the relational sphere, helping to strengthen the relationship between the company and consumers; in particular, referring to innovations in experiential shopping, in customer orientation with the participation of micro-marketing, in "e-tailing" which represents the use of technological tools to establish direct contact as well as interaction with consumers.

Digitization has radically transformed society and has had a distinct impact on the field of retail (Hagberg et al., 2016) (Grewal et al., 2017). Its implications for brick-and-mortar stores are of utmost importance, as the majority of retail sales still take place in physical stores. Digital devices are increasingly populating physical stores and are supplied by retailers or brought in by connected consumers. So rather than separating digitalization from retail, we are now seeing initiatives for the integration of the digital and physical logic of retail. In the digital age, the occurrence of needs, purchases and consumption is much closer in time and space and is naturally integrated into customer online/offline daily routines (Reinartz & Imschloß, 2017) (Grewal et al., 2017).

"Innovation experience" has been identified as playing a central role in how European retailers are changing the industry (Krafft & Mantrala, 2010). Retailers, consequently, need to understand environmental change and behave accordingly (Pantanoa & Timmermansa, 2014), which is driving the introduction of smart technology into retail businesses. Therefore, they must develop the capacity to understand the new competitive scenario enabling innovation and the related action strategy by integrating and reconfiguring internal and external organizational skills, competencies, resources and technologies. It can be affirmed that the system of innovation elements in companies and the growing changes in the retail market stimulate a relational approach between the retailer and the customer to highlight certain characteristics of retail business management that define "relational" proximity (Sansone & Colamatteo, 2017).

4.2.2 A marketing channel approach

A "channel" can be a physical retail store, website, mail order catalogue or direct communication, email or SMS communication. Based on the functionality of a channel, distinction is made between the distribution and the communication structures. A channel structure's functionality usually explains the type of service offered and reflects its purpose and functions (Shareef et al., 2016). From a distribution perspective, it is assumed that the channel structures through which products, services and information are sold to customers are a commodity. This distribution channel can be made up of several intermediaries or it can be directly from the seller to the customer (or contact points). In terms of communication, the channel is used to transmit advertising offers or to transmit the flow of information and to ensure interactivity between the brand and consumers.

A marketing channel is entirely dedicated to carrying out certain activities that ensure the distribution of the product or service to the right customer, at the right time and in the right place, and most efficiently and effectively. Considering the function, composition and interactivity, the extensive use of the marketing channel can be classified into five groups: product, service, information, opinion leaders and reference groups. A marketing channel is traditionally referred to as a distribution channel where the movement of the product from the manufacturer to the end-user is the primary focus. Its functionality and purpose are changing dramatically with the application of the internet and mobile technology. The 21st-century mobile marketing channel has seen radical changes in the structure, function and requirements of the conventional physical channel (Shareef et al., 2016).

An online marketing channel, for distribution or communication, is a systematic and uniform network of agencies and institutions, called a structure made up of different interdependent organizations in the supply chain. This channel could be considered as a single member interconnected to form a structured channel to ensure the movement of a product, service or information; to convey an interactive message; or to pursue and shape attitudes individually or socially from seller or retailer to customers (perhaps through intermediaries) in an effective manner (Shareef et al., 2016).

It has been investigated whether the addition of the internet improves or cannibalizes existing sales channels, for example, brick-and-mortar stores (Herhausen et al., 2015). Of particular interest is Zettelmeyer's (2000) in (Geyskens et al., 2003) work on research characterized by the use of game theory; it analytically derives the effects of the decision to add an internet distribution channel to a conventional channel to measure its effects in terms of profits, drawing attention to the fact that most studies have used perceptual performance measures as opposed to evidence-based measures. Retailers (or brands) tend more to leverage multiple channels to achieve their goals. Despite speculation that "pure players" would prevail and cause the death of traditional stores, physical and virtual channels are found to complement or even merge (Teller et al., 2019). "Synergy" is understood to mean when one channel enhances the effectiveness and efficiency of another in joint actions. The whole is then more than the sum of the parts (2 + 2 = 5), as if the association of channels potentiated the overall performance (Poirel & Bonet Fernandez, 2008) (Gallouj & Gallouj, 2009).

4.2.3 Internet: new market or non-market relationships

In industrial economies, the evolution of distribution systems in mass consumption is marked by the appearance of new forms of sale, and by changes in the organization of points of sale, both in terms of physical supply circuits (logistics) and with the process of formalizing exchange relations with suppliers (purchasing negotiation) (Filser & Paché, 2008). Upset by the introduction of electronic commerce, the distribution channel reveals new intermediation modalities transforming its functioning (Pras, 2012). The development of click and mortar, that is to say, the association of online sales and the operation of "physical" stores, undeniably constitutes one of the major development axes linked to the internet (Filser & Paché, 2008). Modern large-scale distribution remains concentrated in urban or peri-urban areas mainly because of the high purchasing power, household equipment (refrigerators, freezers, cars) and the lack of logistics and transport infrastructure in rural areas and the regions furthest from urban centres (Amine, 2012).

It should be noted that the commercial landscape in emerging countries is characterized by the duality of modern and traditional distribution networks. We note the coexistence of several sales formats: on the one hand, the legal proximity trade (made up of neighbourhood grocery stores, open-air or covered markets at variable intervals) and the informal network of street vendors, parallel markets anchored in local culture and customs, and on the other, the modern network (hypermarkets and supermarkets to limit themselves to food) recently adopted by mainly urban customers. The distribution chain is particularly long in rural areas where a large part of the population generally lives and where small local stalls and permanent or periodic outdoor or covered markets are generally found (Amine, 2012) (Durand et al., 2010). More recently, and after the movement of the relocation of commerce and warehouses to the city outskirts, we are perceiving the ebb of goods towards city centres, through the revival of local commerce as well as the repositioning of logistics units of smaller size, intended to massify orders from small traders and internet users (Durand et al., 2010).

Since the beginning, the potential of the internet as a radically different and highly effective communication channel was evident. But retailers quickly realized its potential to provide information, facilitate two-way communication with customers, collect market research data, promote goods and services, and ultimately support online ordering of goods and provide an extremely rich and flexible new retail channel. It is the internet's "unique ability to generate tangible economic gains" that has been the main catalyst for the explosion of e-commerce activities. In doing so, the internet provides a mechanism for retailers to expand target markets, improve communications with customers, expand product lines, improve profitability, improve customer relationships and deliver personalized offers (Doherty & Ellis-Chadwick, 2010).

Several debates on the extent to which the point of purchase could be moved from the "physical market place" to the "virtual market space" have been carried out (Doherty & Ellis-Chadwick, 2010). Early research presented the internet as a "phenomenal marketing opportunity". Next, it was envisioned that the internet could play an important, but fairly passive, marketing role in deploying clear, interesting and up-to-date web pages to attract customers. Others envisioned a somewhat more proactive role for the internet, in which it enabled one-to-one marketing, facilitating communication with customers on an individualized basis rather than mass marketing. Distribution and communication channels are now essential to any brand or retailer. In a truly synchronized digital marketing place, no channel exists in isolation. Brands will increasingly design fully integrated experiences to meet the needs of well-informed consumers with digital capabilities, thus creating a new retail and electronic communications ecosystem (Anderson et al., 2011).

4.2.4 E-commerce, m-commerce or social commerce

With the advent of the internet, distribution and communication are changing and leading to transformations or the introduction of new sales formats on the one hand, and a change in consumer behaviour on the other. Websites add to a brand's distribution channels, act as a brand's primary channel, or serve other brand purposes. Consumers will interweave their visits to all the points of contact that a brand offers to meet their needs in terms of information acquisition, comparisons, purchases or other tasks. The role of consumers is becoming even more active, thanks to digital platforms. Unlike the first merchant websites, the content of these platforms is mainly produced by internet users, feeding their profiles, that of their friends or that of the brand (Coutant & Stenger, 2012).

The functional aspects and objectives specific to each website category, merchant sites, sites dedicated to the brand or community sites should be emphasized. It is recognized that merchant websites and branded websites pursue significantly different objectives; the first being designed to optimize traffic and sales, while the second being more a matter of information and promotion of the brand, its universe and its products to the general public (Ben Nasr & Trinquecoste, 2015).

In modern environments, brands spread information to get in touch with customers. With the help of technology, they can make more informed decisions about which products or services to consume. Yet not all customer decisions are based on in-depth information research and detailed decision-making processes. Some decisions are spontaneous and quick when shopping online or in stores, and often driven by strategic visual presentations and merchandise assortments designed by the retailer (Grewal et al., 2017) (Littler & Melanthiou, 2006). Mobile commerce includes all activities related to a (potential) business transaction carried out through communication networks that interface with wireless or mobile devices (smartphones) (San-Martín et al., 2015).

In addition to electronic commerce (e-commerce), mobile commerce (m-commerce) is one of the major disruptions in retail, further complicating the retail landscape. However, social commerce, which refers to the sales activity carried out directly through digital social networks, presents a new challenge to traditional distribution channels (Picot-Coupey, 2013). The mobile revolution, coupled with the growth of social media, has created a situation where customers are bringing their entire social network into the store.

This creates new challenges as the retailer has no direct influence over an individual social network that is beyond the control of the retailer's brand or the manufacturer of the product. In this new situation, the importance of an individual relationship between the retailer and the customer is greater, as the customer acts as an intermediary between himself and the wider social network, which is maintained even in the environment in-store via mobile devices (Piotrowicz & Cuthbertson, 2014).

With the rise of e-commerce (Reinartz et al., 2019), the physical store is no longer seen as the main interface with the consumer. The appearance of "click & collect" shops allows consumers to order online and then collect the merchandise from the shop or another collection point designated by the brand (Beck & Rygl, 2015). From a value creation perspective, the physical store, e-commerce, m-commerce and social commerce have become less competitive and more complementary; depending on what the consumer seeks to establish, these formats present several possibilities for carrying out a journey of researching information, sharing, exchanging and purchasing (Picot-Coupey, 2013) at their own pace and in their way. A relationship is renewed thanks to new sales forms, or even mutated sale forms, and leads to changes in frequentation and spending between the consumer and the brand (Badot et al., 2018).

4.2.5 *Social media and social networks*

For Coleman (1990), the social capital, inherent in social structures, brings two types of benefits to actors: the improvement of information flow, and the benevolence of others towards consumers. In other words, the social network also imposes constraints since it carries obligations, standards and sanctions. A "social network" is seen as a mode of coordination of individual activities, an alternative to hierarchy and contract. Social networks make it possible to circulate and especially qualify the information essential to the functioning of the market. Conversely, these market exchanges give rise to the creation of lasting social relations between economic actors (Baret et al., 2006). "Social media" (social media) has changed the way people communicate, collaborate, exchange and connect with others (Labrecque, 2014). Unlike the first merchant websites, the content of these platforms is essentially produced by internet users, feeding their profiles or that of their friends. Participation is at the service of the platform, whose value (commercial and financial) is based on the organization of this participation and then its exploitation (Coutant & Stenger, 2012).

Several terms have been used to describe social networks, such as Web 2.0, Social Web, Community Web, Participatory Web, Participatory Media, sometimes even Community Networks. This indistinct use of a multitude of terms mobilizes heterogeneous conceptual fields and does not facilitate the understanding of the phenomenon. To fill in the "fuzzy" outlines of the term "social networks", the following definition has been proposed: "A group of online applications that are based on the ideology and technology of Web 2.0 and allow the creation and exchange of user-generated content" (Coutant & Stenger, 2012).

Social media provides a medium for direct interaction, which is an ideal environment for creating brand communities, as well as building and strengthening relationships with and better understanding consumers. If the brand wants to avoid the possibility of backlash, comments that could damage its reputation or lose sales opportunities, it should fully understand and analyse the online "environment" (Labrecque, 2014). It appears that in a situation of great uncertainty, only social networks make it possible to circulate and, above all, qualify the information essential to the functioning of the market. Conversely, these market exchanges give rise to the creation of lasting social relations between economic actors (Baret et al., 2006).

Brands and consumers are increasingly present and active online, more specifically on social networks. These become places of meeting, exchange, consultation and, in some countries, commercial transactions; this is how the social and market spheres juxtapose (Badot et al., 2018). Social networks are built around socio-digital platforms and are social forms made up of relationships or interactions between people (Degenne, 2011). These relationships take shape over the telephone or through the internet, for example via Facebook, Instagram, YouTube or other similar platforms.

No matter where the consumer is, in a physical store or online, it is always reassuring to consult their peers or ask those close to them. The members of the group to which a person belongs give him or her more confidence before making any purchases (Badot et al., 2018). Brands equip their stores with tools (such as connected mirrors, digital terminals or photography stands), allowing consumers to have easier and more direct access to their social network. A hashtag that the brand provides to its visitors makes it easier to group (in one place) any information shared which relates to this "code". Members belonging to a community will therefore be responsible for injecting information in addition to messages disseminated by the brand (Okazaki, 2009). Word-of-mouth communications between consumers have become increasingly important as they focus on the positive experiences of the consumer, thus increasing both brand relevance within target groups and customers' desire for the brand (Klein et al., 2016).

Today, hyper-connected and hyper-engaged consumers face a multitude and diversity of distribution and communication channels that allow them not only to receive information but also to exchange, share or inject data. More and more brands are ensuring seamless transitions between different channels they work with, to empower consumers to view information and make purchases "anywhere, anytime, any product" (Viet Ngo et al., 2016); this is the omnichannel mantra.

4.2.6 Multichannel

At the start of the 21st century, the explosion of the internet bubble called into question the web's ability to establish itself as the sole market space (Vanheems, 2012). Today, the internet is an increasingly essential channel for businesses and their customers. It offers brands the possibility of adopting "hybrid system or click & mortar" strategies that lead a customer to move from a store (physical store or drive or other) to the website and vice versa (Filser & Paché, 2008). In addition to physical distribution networks, the internet is positioned as a decisive element in the "development of multi-channel distribution strategies" (Paché et al., 2014). The attractiveness of the physical point of sale could be enhanced by "the excitement of the offer or the location" (Badot, 2015); the latter becomes one of several channels offering sources of inspiration via sharing sites or via social networks (Stassi, 2013).

Developing integrated multichannel retail strategies has listed key challenges in organizational structure, data integration, consumer behaviour analysis and ratings (Beck & Rygl, 2015). Without studying, understanding and evaluating the multichannel environment, operationalizing strategies can present several challenges for brands. Common characteristics of a well-integrated multichannel strategy can include highly integrated promotions, product consistency across channels and an integrated information system that shares customer pricing and inventory data (Doherty & Ellis-Chadwick, 2010) (Beck & Rygl, 2015) (Ghose &

odri-Adamopoulos, 2016). However, this process depends on how the channels interact and how customers perceive them. In this sense, it is considered that a brand's multiple channels are part of a coherent whole and creator of value (Paché et al., 2014).

The emergence of non-traditional shopping channels attests to the growing importance of cross-channel retail. In this context, the point of sale could fulfil a function of "relay in a purchasing process", a function of a "showroom" or a function of "geo-localized satisfaction" of consumers' impulses, or it could "produce value" following an internet purchase (Stassi, 2013). A consumer now has more possibilities to make purchases either with the same retailer present in different channels or with different retailers in different channels (Kwon & Jain, 2009). While there has been a lot of positive talk about the virtues of multichannel retailing, there are still dissenting voices who believe that retailers still have a long way to go before they "get it right" (actually get it right) (Doherty & Ellis-Chadwick, 2010).

The establishment of a multichannel distribution structure, by increasing the number of points of contact, has become an essential requirement for retail chains. The use of common infrastructures, the establishment of joint operations and marketing policies, and the sharing of customers are all possible sources of synergies between distribution channels. An extensive commercial presence also represents an opportunity for a brand to increase the opportunities for contact with its customers, to offer them a better level of service and, thus, to promote their retention (Nicholson & Vanheems, 2009).

Among the new channels that enrich the points of contact between a brand and consumers, there are the drive and ephemeral stores. The drive is establishing itself as a natural consequence of the evolution of sales formats and is part of the multichannel development logic of distribution networks (Vy & Cliguet, 2016). Ephemeral stores, considered to be the most recent expression of innovative solutions, are managed alone or can be combined with other brand channels, and this at a local or international level (Picot-Coupey, 2012).

In a multichannel context, risks of conflicts could arise between the different channels adopted by a brand or a brand. Among the most important are intensity, importance, extent and dynamics (Angelmar, 1988). By conflict intensity, we mean the "magnitude" that exists between the different channels as all conflicting objects do not have the same stakes for the parties. The notion of importance is generally defined as the consequences for each channel. General conflict literature emphasizes the extent of the conflict, that is, the number of objects the conflict is about. Scope plays a critical role in the escalation of a conflict when parties open "new fronts" in it. But taking into account new objects can also facilitate an agreement by defining a "package" which allows each party to improve its situation overall.

Retailers are having to deal with new purchasing behaviours to meet consumer demands without sacrificing their business model due to logistical complexity. The coordination of online and traditional channels becomes even more important (Hübner et al., 2015). Consumers exhibit migratory behaviour within the multichannel space. One might think that the migrations that take place from the brand's store to a newly established website are a reflection of an evolution of the whole evoked. The establishment of a merchant website by a physically established brand is, in fact, theoretically likely to affect consumers (Van Baal & Dach, 2005). Customers who buy through online channels lack first-hand product experience, which makes product selection riskier. In an omnichannel environment, where there is no distinction between channels, consumers have the opportunity to research product information online, and visit stores to assess alternatives and learn more about the products before making their final purchase decision (Bernon et al., 2016).

4.2.7 The omnichannel

Although retailers have heavily invested in e-commerce operations to complement their physical stores, the economics facing these hybrid retailers remain daunting. For those who operate both stores and websites, the conventional "omnichannel" strategy is to encourage shopping across all channels so that consumers who only buy from stores start shopping online, too, and vice versa. Moreover, getting consumers to the physical point of sale could produce significant returns due to the stimuli and experiences offered on the spot.

> If customers come to (physical) stores regularly, brands shouldn't be encouraging them to buy online. The most profitable game is to persuade online shoppers to come down to the store, where the environment can entice them to spend more: This qualifies as a winning omnichannel strategy.
>
> (Zeng et al., 2016)

Omnichannel is defined as a synchronized operating model in which all of the company's channels are aligned and present a unique face to the consumer, as well as a consistent way of doing business (Bernon et al., 2016).

The omnichannel concept is seen as an evolution of the multichannel concept (Piotrowicz & Cuthbertson, 2014). While multichannel implies a division between the physical store and the online store, with the omnichannel, consumers move freely between the online store, mobile phones and the physical store, all within the same transaction process (Beck & Rygl, 2015). Communication channels and social networks are added to the "traditional" physical channels and online channels. Customers who were once disturbed by increasingly complex offers know how to take advantage of them; they tend to consume according to their needs, to access offers and services everywhere, all the time (Carteron, 2013).

The share of online sales in retail is growing globally; it is being influenced by increased sales in existing online channels, as well as the continued entry of brick-and-mortar retailers into e-commerce. As retail moves towards a seamless omnichannel shopping experience, the distinctions between physical stores and online stores will disappear. This omnichannel revolution was sparked by the recent reaction of brick-and-mortar retailers to new service offerings from pure online retailers. The majority of these retailers, therefore, now serve customers through multiple sales channels. In addition, remote retailers, such as pure players, establish physical stores, temporary or fixed, to expand their service offerings (Hübner et al., 2015).

The current omnichannel environment therefore demands a satisfying and personalized experience through all the interactions of available channels for the consumer's use during their purchasing journey: customers start their journey anywhere, anytime and from any device (Melero et al., 2016). ROPO (research online, purchase offline) refers to the behaviour of omnichannel consumers (Carteron, 2013); in this context, their journeys must be fluid and must provide a homogeneous, unified (Bernon et al., 2016) and transparent (Melero et al., 2016; Sopadjieva et al., 2017) customer experience, whatever channel is used (Piotrowicz & Cuthbertson, 2014). Shall a brand operate in an omnichannel context, it will operationalize a multitude of retail formats, online and offline, physical and temporal, to provide customers with a seamless shopping experience.

Table 4.2 synthesizes retail's evolution in three phases, and for each phase, different causes of disruption causing that "change" are identified.

Table 4.2 The main causes of disruption in retail

The three main phases in the evolution of retail	Retail disruptions (Grewal et al., 2010)	Distribution, market and exchange (FlexEngage, n.d.)	The retail metamorphosis[a]
The past	The first disruption begins with the birth of the internet (1994). The second disruption in 1995 marked the sale of the first online book by Amazon.	Retail is driven by the market: Retail as an organized industry started in the 18th and 19th centuries with the rise of urban covered markets, speciality stores and department stores. In the late 1800s, Montgomery Ward developed the catalogues that allowed consumers to shop without leaving home. The phone made it possible to make impulse purchases later. Physical brands: the beginnings of retail marketing about signage and packaging, which could inform customers about the quality and style of a product. As retail marketing has developed, retailers focused on the elements of the marketing mix: the 4Ps (product, price, location and promotion) to sell their products. Marketing decisions were made based on market research such as surveys and focus groups, to better understand the customer. Advertising tools such as billboards, direct mail or others have developed subsequently.	Until the advent of the internet, retail focused on the interaction between retailer and consumer. 1700–1800: "Mom-and-pop stores" is a colloquial term for a small independent family business. Although these multi-purpose stores (as they offer a combination of groceries, drugstores or toys) are less common, family businesses are present to this day. 1800–1900: At the end of the 19th century and the beginning of the 20th century, the economic and commercial sectors (of the United States) changed dramatically. Agriculture, which was previously the dominant activity, has been replaced by manufacturing and industry. Institutions (such as Macy's (1858), Bloomingdales (1861) and Sears (1886)) have become staples in consumers' lives, influencing what they will buy, how they will furnish their homes and what luxury products they will need. These department stores didn't just sell items. They provided demonstrations, lectures and entertainment events.

1883: The first cash register was invented by James Ritty. Before that, many businesses struggled to keep track of their books and were often unsure whether they were operating at a profit or a loss.
During this phase or this "old order of retail", supply was limited and prices high[b].

The concept of shopping malls began in the 20th century. It was envisioned as a cultural and social centre where people could come together and not only do their shopping but also make it an activity.
The one-stop shop: While people liked malls for the social aspect and the pleasure of window shopping and going from store to store, there was also a resurgence of interest in a "one-stop shop" return. However, unlike the general stores, these department stores served larger populations and provided low-cost items on a much larger scale (Walmart, Kmart, and Target opened their stores in 1962).

Checks and cash: Regardless of the method of payment, the core of the exchange was to exchange something of "agreed value for something the customer wants".
Money, cash, paper checks and hand-held credit books were the means of exchanging currency for commodities.
Without these payment vehicles, consumers could not make a purchase (or make an exchange); they should wait until they can afford it or should just buy what is needed.
The cross channel: At the time, online selling was considered a risky and avant-garde concept, but has become an essential channel.
Beginning in the 1990s, "online stores" allowed consumers to browse and purchase items. The development of this channel was considered as a threat to traditional stores (brick and mortars). In the context of multichannelling, brands see online stores as complementary to traditional stores.

The present

The sixth disruption; the birth of social networks in 2007.
The adoption of "smartphones" in 2009 marked the seventh disruption.

(*Continued*)

The three main phases in the evolution of retail	*Retail disruptions (Grewal et al., 2010)*	*Distribution, market and exchange (FlexEngage, n.d.)*	*The retail metamorphosis[a]*
	The ninth disruption represents the increase in the popularity of "big data" in 2013.	The availability of information online has also contributed to the formation of consumer attitudes. No longer depending on ad hoc information written by the brand and disseminated through traditional vehicles, consumers have access to information at any time via their computer or mobile phone. Data-driven segmentation: "Big data" is driving changes in the way retailers market their products to consumers. The availability of data allows retailers to highlight specific customer profiles. Segmentation then allows retailers to create targeted sales strategies that meet the needs and experiences of these different groups. Payment by credit: In the 1920s, credit cards began to take hold of the American buyer. The first universal credit card that could be used in multiple establishments was the Diners Club card in 1950.	The 90s and the beginning of online commerce: The growth of electronic commerce mirrored the growth of the internet. Initially, some people were sceptical about providing personal data and payment information online, but the development of the SSL security protocol in the 1990s helped allay those fears. Promising opportunities; social networks: In 2011, Facebook rolled out sponsored articles as a form of early advertising. Marketers could take advantage of the sheer amount of data people provide to Facebook to target very specific customers. Today, Facebook and Instagram are also channelling where brands can sell their products directly. Giant "retailers" transformed commerce when they were able to offer important choices at very low prices. These sales formats have been very damaging to small traders.

Credit cards: The first credit cards didn't see the light of day until the 1940s, when banks and retailers began to introduce plastic credit cards.
Bank of America's "BankAmericard", launched in 1958, was the first successful credit card. Credit cards are convenient for customers and good for retailers, as consumers tend to spend more when using their credit cards.

Even if the consumer does not have the means to perform an act of exchange, purchasing utilizing a credit card allows him to obtain the desired product instantly, provided the amount is paid on the due date.

Between the years 2010 and 2015, business stagnated while customer satisfaction declined and online spending increased. Low tech costs will help young brands have a better chance of survival in the market[c].

| The future | The tenth disruption, that of the development of "blockchain", from the start to the end of 2017. | Online stores cannot offer internet users a sensory experience in which they can immerse themselves. This presents itself as a challenge for retailers operating only online.
Consumers are shopping in stores and online. Even though they use the internet to research and compare prices, they still want the experience of touching and trying a physical product.
Retailers are increasingly using technologies such as augmented reality, interactive video, 360 views and gesture controls to bring products to life on shoppers' screens, and this will only grow in the future. | We are talking about "cross-channel" viscosity, a strategy which should represent the current commerce of tomorrow and which consists of articulating physical channels and electronic channels to serve the consumer as close as possible to his space-time constraints, "any time anywhere, any device", any cloud (ATAWADAC) (Badot, 2015). More recently, retailers are talking about a "seamless shopping experience", a flawless shopping experience (Bernon et al., 2016) (Beck & Rygl, 2015). |

(Continued)

The three main phases in the evolution of retail	*Retail disruptions (Grewal et al., 2010)*	*Distribution, market and exchange (FlexEngage, n.d.)*	*The retail metamorphosis[a]*
		The purely personalized segment: The segment of the future is a "Segment of One" (one person is targeted). Individual consumers can be identified and targeted based not only on their consumer profile (including loyalty data and purchase histories) but also on their precise location (provided by GPS on mobile phones). Cashless/blockchain payment: Retail payments are at the forefront of digital disruption today, with consumer demand pushing retailers to be the first to adopt emerging technologies in digital payments. In the future, blockchain is expected to play an increasing role in retail payments, as the big banks learn how to harness distributed ledger technology. The general trend driving the shift in retail payments is that consumers want payment transactions to go away. The less they have to think about paying, the less friction there is in the process, the more likely they are to complete a purchase and come back to a retailer to buy again.	The "phygital" consumer: the consumer is "hyper-connected" and his life is rather driven by digital technology. He buys when he wants, where he wants and how he wants; this makes this customer journey more complicated than ever for brands/retailers. The multitude of points of contact that the retailer can make available to consumers allows him to live an "omni-experience" while eliminating the "pain points" which may be the cause of the latter's dissatisfaction. With the "phygital", shopping becomes a simple, fast, practical and transparent experience (Ter Haar, 2020). Retail is entering a new era of commerce. Flexibility, data and intelligence will help businesses dive into customer-centric commerce. Despite its development, the upheaval of physical commerce refers to convenience stores (Sansone & Colamatteo, 2017).

The economic crisis and changing consumer lifestyles have caused independent and associated retailers to reinterpret their format by thinking of a basket of attributes, which includes other services to meet better consumer needs.

Today, people are looking for content and experiences in their shopping activities that can influence what they buy. In 2019, brands succeeded in creating strong business experiences based on content and experience[d].

To bridge the cycle, "tech-companies" will dominate the market; these small specialized entities will take over and evacuate the trade giants from the value chain[e].

a https://www.bigcommerce.com/blog/retail/#the-history-and-evolution-of-retail-stores
b https://www.cbmsolution.com/Resources/Articles/evolution-and-future-transformation-of-local-business
c https://www.cbmsolution.com/Resources/Articles/evolution-and-future-transformation-of-local-business
d https://www.bigcommerce.com/blog/retail/#the-history-and-evolution-of-retail-stores
e https://www.cbmsolution.com/Resources/Articles/evolution-and-future-transformation-of-local-business

Some consider the evolution of "retail" as a response to environmental challenges in different ways, such as launching new sales formats or improving costs or management processes (Grewal et al., 2010). This development has also caused upheavals in marketing, communication and the shopping experience. Retail formats are therefore tools allowing brands to meet consumer expectations.

References

Amine, A., 2012. La grande distribution dans les pays émergents: caractéristiques, enjeux et perspectives. *Marché et organisations*, 1(15), pp. 117–141.

Anderson, M., Buckner, N. & Eikelmann, S., 2011. The M-Commerce challenge to retail. *Strategy + Business*, 62, pp. 1–5.

Angelmar, R., 1988. *Les conflits dans les canaux de distribution*. Fontainebleau: INSEAD.

Antéblian, B. & Filser, M., 2008. Nouvelles formes de commercialisation au détail des fruits et légumes: du format du point de vente aux enjeux logistiques. *Logistique & Management*, 16(2), pp. 45–56.

Badot, O., 2015. *Tendances Retail*. s.l.: s.n.

Badot, O., Lemoine, J.-F. & Ochs, A., 2018. *Distribution 4.0*. 1st ed. s.l.: Pearson.

Baret, C., Huault, I. & Picq, T., 2006. Management et réseaux sociaux Jeux d'ombres et de lumières sur les organisations. *Revue Française de Gestion*, 4(163), pp. 93–106.

Beck, N. & Rygl, D., 2015. Categorization of multiple channel retailing in Multi-, Cross-, and Omni-Channel Retailing for retailers and retailing. *Journal of Retailing and Consumer Services*, 27, pp. 170–178.

Ben Nasr, I. & Trinquecoste, J.-F., 2015. À propos des routes cognitives et affectives de l'e-satisfaction et de l'attitude: Les comportements utilitaires et expérientiels empruntent-ils le même itinéraire? *Management & Avenir*, 8(82), pp. 55–181.

Bernon, M., Cullen, J. & Gorst, J., 2016. Online retail returns management. Integration within an omnichannel distribution context. *International Journal of Physical Distribution & Logistics Management*, 46(6/7), pp. 584–605.

Botschen, G. & Wegerer, P. K., 2017. Brand-driven retail format innovation: A conceptual framework. *International Journal of Retail & Distribution Management*, 45(7/8), pp. 874–891.

Bradley, G. & LaFleur, E., 2016. Toward the development of hedonic-utilitarian measures of retail service. *Journal of Retailing and Consumer Services*, 32, pp. 60–66.

Brown, S., 1990. The wheel of retailing: Past and future. *Journal of Retailing*, Summer, 66(2), pp. 143–149.

Carteron, V., 2013. Expérience client et distribution « omnicanale ». *L'Expansion Management Review*, 2(149), pp. 25–35.

Chanut, O. & Paché, G., 2013. L'avenir incertain des marques de distributeurs. *L'Expansion Management Review*, 3(138), pp. 10–21.

Chevrel, C. (2012). Une histoire des grands magasins. [Online] Available at: http://sabf.fr/hist/arti/sabf193.php [Accessed 03 05 2020].

Coutant, A. & Stenger, T., 2012. Les médias sociaux: une histoire de participation. *Le Temps des médias*, 1(18), pp. 76–86.

Cundiff, E. W., 1965. Concepts in comparative retailing. *The Journal of Marketing*, January, 29(1), pp. 59–63.

De Lassus, C., 2012. Les pop-up stores de luxe: entre lieu mythique et endroit éphémère, une analyse sémiotique. *Colloque Etienne Thil*, Lille, France, Oct.

Degenne, A., 2011. Retour à l'analyse des réseaux sociaux. Entretien réalisé par Thomas Stenger et Alexandre Coutant. *Hermès*, 1(59), pp. 39–42.

Doherty, N. F. & Ellis-Chadwick, F., 2010. Internet retailing: The past, the present and the future. *International Journal of Retail & Distribution Management*, 38(11/12), pp. 943–965.

Doubman, J. R., 1935. What is new in retailing? *American Marketing Journal*, April, 2(2), pp. 88–91.

Durand, B., Gonzalez-Féliu, J. & Henriot, F., 2010. La logistique urbaine, facteur clé de développement du B to C. *Logistique & Management*, 18(2), pp. 7–19.

Edward Spragg, J., 2017. Articulating the fashion product life-cycle. *Journal of Fashion Marketing and Management: An International Journal*, 21(4), pp. 499–511.

Erdener, K. & Cavusgil, T., 1982. The evolution of food retailing systems: Contrasting the experience of developed and developing countries. *Journal of the Academy of Marketing Science*, 10(3), pp. 249–269.

Evans, J. R., 2011. Retailing in perspective: The past is a prologue to the future. *The International Review of Retail, Distribution and Consumer Research*, 21(1), pp. 1–31.

Felipe, B. S., n.d. Punto de venta. pp. 51–53.

Filser, M. & Paché, G., 2008. La dynamique des canaux de distribution. Approches théoriques et ruptures stratégiques. *Revue Française de gestion*, 2(182), pp. 109–133.

FlexEngage, n.d. The Evolution of Retail: A Look Back and a Look Ahead. [Online] Available at: https://www.flexengage.com/all-posts/retail-evolution [Accessed 28 02 2020].

Gallouj, C. & Gallouj, S., 2009. L'innovation dans la grande distribution: essai de construction d'une approche servicielle. *Management & Avenir*, 1(21), pp. 103–120.

Geyskens, I., Gielens, K. & Dekimpe, M. G., 2003. Comment le marché évalue-t-il l'ajout d'un canal de distribution sur Internet? *Recherche et Applications en Marketing*, 18(2), pp. 101–128.

Ghose, A. & Todri-Adamopoulos, V., 2016. Toward a digital attribution model: measuring the impact of display advertising on online consumer behavior. *MIS Quarterly*, 40(4), pp. 889–910.

Gibbs, A., 1987. Retail innovation in planning. *Progress in Planning*, 27, pp. 1–67.

Grewal, D., Krishnan, R., Levy, M. & Munger, J., 2010. *Retail success and key drivers, in retailing in the 21st century: Current and future trends*. s.l.: Springer-Verlag.

Grewal, D., Roggeveen, A. L. & Nordfält, J., 2017. The Future of Retailing. Journal of Retailing, 91(1), pp. 1–6.

Hagberg, J., Sundstrom, M. & Egels-Zandén, N., 2016. The digitalization of retailing: An exploratory framework. *International Journal of Retail & Distribution Management*, 44(7), pp. 694–712.

Herhausen, D., Binder, J., Schoegel, M. & Herrmann, A., 2015. Integrating bricks with clicks: Retailer-level and channel-level outcomes of online–offline channel integration. *Journal of Retailing*, 91(2), pp. 309–325.

Hollander, S. C., 1960. The wheel of retailing. *The Journal of Marketing*, July, 25(1), pp. 37–42.

Hollander, S. C., 1996. The wheel of retailing. What makes skilled managers succumb to the «prosper mature and decay' pattern»? *Marketing Management*, Summer, 5(2), pp. 63–66.

Hübner, A., Holzapfel, A. & Kuhn, H., 2015. Operations management in multichannel retailing: An exploratory study. *Springer Science+Business Media New York*, 8, pp. 84–100.

Hübner, A., Holzapfel, A. & Kuhn, H., 2016. Distribution systems in omnichannel retailing. *Business Research*, 9, pp. 255–296.

Ingene, A., 2014. Retail evolution: Historical facts, theoretical logic and critical thinking. *Journal of Historical Research in Marketing*, 6(2), pp. 279–299.

Keri, D., 1998. Applying evolutionary models to the retail sector. *The International Review of Retail, Distribution and Consumer Research*, 8(2), pp. 65–181.

Klein, J. F., Falk, T., Esch, F.-R. & Gloukhovtsev, A., 2016. Linking pop-up brand stores to brand experience and word of mouth: The case of luxury retail. *Journal of Business Research*, 69(12), pp. 5761–5767.

Krafft, M. & Mantrala, M., 2010. *Retailing in the 21st century*. s.l.: Springer.

Kwon, K.-N. & Jain, D., 2009. Multichannel shopping through nontraditional retail formats: Variety-seeking behavior with hedonic and utilitarian motivations. *Journal of Marketing Channels*, 16, pp. 49–168.

Labrecque, L. I., 2014. Fostering consumer brand relationships in social media environments: The role of parasocial interaction. *Journal of Interactive Marketing*, 28, pp. 134–148.

Lemaitre, N. & De Barnier, V., 2015. Quand le consommateur devient commerçant: Motivations, production d'expérience et perspectives. *Décisions Marketing*, 28(2), pp. 11–28.

Lipkin, M., 2016. Customer experience formation in today's service landscape. *Journal of Service Management*, 27(5), pp. 678–703.

Littler, D. & Melanthiou, D., 2006. Consumer perceptions of risk and uncertainty and the implications for behaviour towards innovative retail services: The case of Internet Banking. *Journal of Retailing and Consumer Services*, 13, pp. 431–443.

Lowson, R. H., 2005. Retail operations strategies. Empirical evidence of role, competitive contribution and life cycle. *International Journal of Operations & Production Management*, 25(7), pp. 642–680.

Malhotra, J., 2007. Retail matrix: A strategic tool for performance analysis of retail formats. *IIMB Management Review*, pp. 365–374.

Marciniak, R. & Budnarowska, C., 2018. *Exploration of pop-up retail: The department store perspective*. Belgium, 4th International colloquium on design, branding and marketing (ICDBM).

McArthur, E., Weaven, S. & Dant, R., 2016. The evolution of retailing: A meta review of the literature. *Journal of Macromarketing*, 36(3), pp. 272–286.

McNair, M. P. & May, E. G., 1978. The next revolution of the retailing wheel. *Harvard Business Review*, pp. 81–91.

Melero, I., Sese, J. & Verhoef, P., 2016. Recasting the customer experience in today's omnichannel environment. *Universia Business Review*, 50, pp. 18–37.

Miotto, A. P. & Gomes Parente, J., 2015. Retail evolution model in emerging markets: Apparel store formats in Brazil. *International Journal of Retail & Distribution Management*, 43(3), pp. 242–260.

Nicholson, P. & Vanheems, R., 2009. Orientations d'achat et comportement multicanal du client. *Management & Avenir*, 1(21), pp. 136–156.

Niehm, L. S., Ann Marie, F., Jeong, M. & Kim, H.-J., 2007. Pop-up retail's acceptability as an innovative business strategy and enhancer of the consumer shopping experience. *Journal of Shopping Center Research*, 13(7), pp. 1–30.

Novak, M., 2010. *The evolution of the retail landscape*. s.l.: Western University. Graduate & Postdoctoral Studies.

Okazaki, S., 2009. The tactical use of mobile marketing: How adolescents' social networking can best shape brand extentions. *Journal of Advertising Research*, 49(1), pp. 12–26.

Paché, G., Seck, A. M. & Fulconis, F., 2014. Quels bénéfices peut retirer l'entreprise d'un management multicanal intégratif? *La Revue des Sciences de Gestion*, 5(269–270), pp. 55–63.

Paddison, R., Findlay, A. M. & Dawson, J., 1990. *Retailing in less developed countries. An introduction*. London: Routledge.

Pantano, E. & Dennis, C., 2017. Exploring the origin of retail stores in Europe: Evidence from southern Italy from the 6th century BCE to the 3d century BCE. *Journal of Retailing and Customer Services*, 39, pp. 243–249.

Pantanoa, E. & Timmermansa, H., 2014. *What is smart for retailing?* s.l., 12th International Conference on Design and Decision Support Systems in Architecture and Urban Planning, DDSS 2014.

Picot-Coupey, K., 2012. Pop-up stores and the international development of retail networks. *International marketing trends conference*, Venice, Italy.

Picot-Coupey, K., 2013. Les voies d'avenir du magasin physique à l'heure du commerce connecté. *Gestion*, 38(2), pp. 51–61.

Piotrowicz, W. & Cuthbertson, R., 2014. Introduction to the special issue information technology in retail: Toward omnichannel retailing. *International Journal of Electronic Commerce*, 18(4), pp. 5–15.

Poirel, C. & Bonet Fernandez, D., 2008. La stratégie de distribution multiple. *Revue Française de Gestion*, 2(182), pp. 155–170.

Pras, B., 2012. La résilience du marketing. *Revue Française de Gestion*, 9(228/229), pp. 59–85.

Rao, S., 2009. Concept of life cycle in retail. *Sales/Marketing Management*.

Reinartz, W. & Imschloß, M., 2017. From point of sale to point of need: How digital technology is transforming retailing. *The Future of Retailing*, 9(1), 42–47.

Reinartz, W., Wiegand, N. & Imschloss, M., 2019. The impact of digital transformation on the retailing value chain. *International Journal of Research in Marketing*, 36, pp. 355–366.

Reynolds, J., Howard, E., Cuthbertson, C. & Hristov, L., 2007. Perspectives on retail format innovation: Relating theory and practice. *International Journal of Retail & Distribution Management*, 35(8), pp. 647–660.

Rieunier, S. & Volle, P., 2002. Tendances de consommation et stratégies de différenciation des distributeurs. *Décisions Marketing*, 27, pp. 19–30.

Rousey, S. P. & Morganosky, M. A., 1996. Retail format change in US markets. *International Journal of Retail & Distribution Management*, 24(3), pp. 8–16.

San-Martín, S., López-Catalán, B. & Ramón-Jerónimo, M. A., 2015. Signalling as a means to generate loyalty in m-commerce: Does shopper experience moderate the process? *Journal of Customer Behavior*, 14(3), pp. 235–256.

Sansone, M. & Colamatteo, A., 2017. Trends and dynamics in retail industry: Focus on relational proximity. *International Business Research*, 10(2), pp. 169–179.

Senkel, M.-P., 2002. Coordination logistique et fonctionnement du canal de distribution. *Revue Française du Marketing*, 3(188), pp. 79–89.

Shankar, V. & Yadav, M., 2011. Innovations in retailing. *Journal of Retailing*, 87, pp. S1–S2.

Shareef, M. A., Dwivedi, Y. K. & Kumar, V., 2016. *Mobile marketing channel. Online consumer behavior.* Springer briefs in business ed. s.l.: Springer.

Slywotzky, A., Christensen, C. M., Tedlow, R. S. & Carr, N. G., 2000. The future of commerce. *Harvard Business Review*, pp. 1–20.

Sopadjieva, E., Dholakia, U. M. & Benjamin, B., 2017. *A study of 46,000 shoppers shows that omnichannel retailing works.* [Online] Available at: hbr.org/2017/01/a-study-of-46000-shoppers-shows-that-omnichannel-retailling-works [Accessed 15 02 2018].

Sorescu, A. et al., 2011. Innovations in retail business models. *Journal of Retailing*, 87, pp. S3–S16.

Stassi, F., 2013. *Le web et les magasins sont devenus interconnectés et complémentaires.* [Online] Available at: www.businessmarches.com [Accessed 20 Octobre 2017].

Teller, C., Brusset, X. & Kotzab, H., 2019. Physical and digital market places –Where marketing meets operations. *International Journal of Retail & Distribution Management*, 47(12), pp. 1225–1231.

Ter Haar, F., 2020. *Ebeltoft Group.* [Online] Available at: https://ebeltoftgroup.com/blog/phygital-in-retail [Accessed 01 03 2020].

Tibben-Lembke, R. S., 2002. Life after death: Reverse logostics and the product life cycle. *International Journal of Physical Distribution & Logistics Management*, 32(3/4), pp. 223–244.

Van Baal, S. & Dach, C., 2005. Free riding and customer retention across retailers' channels. *Journal of Interactive Marketing*, 19(2), pp. 75–85.

Vandaele, M., 1986. Le cycle de vie du produit: concepts, modèles et évolutions. *Recherche et Applications en Marketing*, 1(2), pp. 75–87.

Vanheems, R., 2012. Multicanalisation des enseignes. Comment internet transforme les comportements en magasin. *Revue Française de Gestion*, 8(227), pp. 13–29.

Viet Ngo, L. et al., 2016. Perceptions of others, mindfulness, and brand experience in retail service setting. *Journal of Retailing and Consumer Services*, 33, pp. 43–52.

Vy, D. & Cliguet, G., 2016. Le drive et la couverture territoriale des réseaux de distribution. *Revue Française de Marketing*, 4/4(258), pp. 29–42.

Wadinambiaratchi, G. H. & Girvan, C., 1972. Theories of retail development. *Social and Economic Studies*, 21(4), pp. 391–403.

Watson, A., Kirby, D. A. & Egan, J., 2002. Franchising, retailing and the development of e-commerce. *International Journal of Retail & Distribution Management*, 30(5), pp. 228–237.

Woodruffe-Burton, H., 2001. Towards a theory of shopping: A holistic framework. *Journal of Consumer Behavior*, 1(3), pp. 256–266.

Zeng, F., Luo, X., Dou, Y. & Zhang, Y., 2016. How to make the most of omnichannel retailing. Your best bet is to get online customers to visit your stores. *Harvard Business Review*, pp. 22–23.

Conclusion

The end of the industrial age has led to modernity; later on, the advent of the information age shaped the society that we know today. Postmodernity refers to a structural change in the individual and in the society that has undergone this change (Decrop, 2008). It highlights emotions and sensations in consumption and is directed to the stimuli that will cause immediate enjoyment in the individual. Once named consumer, the postmodern individual becomes an active agent and participates in the construction of his experience through fragmented processes. More than ever, the consumer is egocentric, tends to relate to himself or others, but only for a brief, present moment (Badot et al., 2018) and not worrying about the future moments. A broad narrative of mobility, fluidity, liquidity has become central to social science research. It has also been theorized that we are witnessing a paradigm shift from a "static social science" to a "mobile science" which redirects the search for the static structures of the modern world towards a "liquefaction" of social structures, institutions, organizations. As a result, mobility, liquidity and transience generate an obsession with novelty, which only the fullness of consumer choice can satisfy (Pomodoro, 2013).

Postmodern society: hyper-real, spiritual and transitory

The so-called postmodern society is in an ideological break with the modern values of progress, linearity, evolution towards a better world of collective utopias, of the power of science; this society no longer has idols or taboos. In response to consumer needs, postmodern society is thinking of new ways of managing their behaviour. It no longer dwells on the "tyranny of details" but presents the fewest constraints and as many private choices as possible;

this is referred to as "hyper choice".[1] In addition to the range of choices that a postmodern society puts forward, many other elements characterize it: hyperreality (Decrop, 2008), fragmentation, decentralization, the reversibility of consumption and production and juxtaposition (Camus & Poulain, 2008).

It is in the hyper-real and transient environment (Pomodoro, 2013), in which the consumer is immersed, that the transformation of reality happens. This is different from objective reality and leads to "the confusion of the true, the false, the sacred and the profane" (Camus & Poulain, 2008). Also, a transient environment produces an attachment to renewal, to the insatiable desire to have new objects to admire and to consume momentarily (Pomodoro, 2013). Authors refer to the "libidinal" economy (Kozinets et al., 2017) as the one driven and fuelled by postmodern consumer desires and the one that serves the proper functioning of the consumer culture. The consumer will actively appropriate and change images while expressing a de-contextualization and disunity of formatted benchmarks. He will experience each situation as if each one should convey a different image of himself and which each time requires specific products; the production of his identity will therefore be conditioned by the products he uses. This is how the postmodern individual changes his image and adapts to new roles constantly and becomes more of a "creator of value" than a "destroyer of value" (Camus & Poulain, 2008).

As a result, mobility, liquidity and ephemerality generate an obsession with novelty, such that only the fullness of choice can satisfy consumers. It is a hypermodern and ephemeral age (Sachdeva & Goel, 2015) which accelerates the appetite for novelty and stimulation through the heterogeneous and growing presentation of offers, products and services; this only increases the opportunities for personal choice. Even more, life will be organized around volatile consumption, guided by seduction and organized around fleeting desires (Pomodoro, 2013) (Decrop, 2008).

The postmodern consumer: in pursuit of memorable and ephemeral experiences

Today's society encourages interactive consumption (Michaud-Trévinal, 2011), "disproportionate and extravagant", and emphasizes the experience of another self (De Lassus & Freire, 2014). It has forced individuals to be informed, to embrace novelty and to assert their subjective preferences (Pomodoro, 2013; Sachdeva & Goel, 2015). The framework of environmental psychology considers shopping to be a "co-constructed global experience", integrating both emotions and appropriation behaviours at the individual and social levels[2] (Michaud-Trévinal, 2011).

The current postmodern consumer (Sachdeva & Goel, 2015) desires to live new experiences (De Lassus & Freire, 2014), memorable (Klein et al., 2016) and rewarding experiences that stimulate their senses, touch their hearts and stimulate their minds (Chen & Fiore, 2017). He is a mobile and flexible individual with a fluctuating personality and tastes, without deep and rooted attachment (Sachdeva & Goel, 2015); he is able to reduce rigidities and resistance and engenders a positive attitude towards innovation. Experiential marketing offers an answer to the existential desire of today's consumer. As opposed to the simple purchase of products or services, it emphasizes his immersion in the consumption experience (Russo Spena et al., 2012). From this perspective, it has been stressed that entertainment is a key element for the satisfaction of the consumer's desire for pleasure and satisfaction, provided that the strict focus on entertainment does not trivialize the consumption experience.

Ephemeral stores are the epitome of today's culture that strives for change, speed and the short attention spans consumers can afford. Overall, ephemeral stores fit into the entertainment economy and the experience economy, as they aim to surprise consumers with temporary "performances" (Overdiek, 2017). That these formats are based on surprise, exclusivity and discovery is a response well suited to current consumer expectations. They fit well with the new models of the postmodern (Picot-Coupey, 2012) and uncertain economy models.

These stores exploit the current "zeitgeist" (Marciniak & Budnarowska, 2018) and appeal to consumers because of the uniqueness of their retail concepts. Moreover, ephemeral stores highlight the hedonic novelty benefits that customers could have access to, rather than addressing mere utilitarian benefits such as facilitating purchasing decisions. Although e-commerce is becoming more present and the future of the physical store is less clear, it is certain that individuals still want to see, smell, touch and try the product, as well as take ownership in a physical point of sale's atmosphere (Piotrowicz & Cuthbertson, 2014), where they freely live temporary and exciting experiences, or even, "portions" of experience (Pomodoro, 2013) (Figure 5.1).

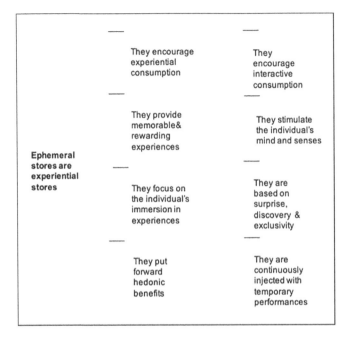

Figure 5.1 Ephemeral stores are experiential stores.

The "prosumer" and the "non-consumer"

In the context of postmodernity, the act of consumption is oriented towards a logic of self-reflection, of personal accomplishment or of a means of forging social bonds. The eight "current consumption" trends (Rieunier & Volle, 2002) have been identified to go in this direction. Fulfilment, personalization, social connection, urgency, emotions, nostalgia, reassurance and simplicity are consumed today. It is observed that the current individual has a desire to "find his swing" and thus forge a "personal morality" referring to ideologies. Through the act of consumption, the individual seeks to bridge his isolation or disconnection to create social bonds.

Although the individual has more free time on his hands or even "chosen" time, he experiences a feeling of running out of time and finds himself facing a more complex world in which he feels uprooted. The current consumption trend calls for playful, stimulating and sensual activities, even regressive trends reflected in relaunched or revisited products or services. Finally, the individual is faced with complex and over-choice proposals: technological offers (Rieunier & Volle, 2002; Hagberg et al., 2016) and product proposals that provide more assurance or security.

To portray this contemporary consumer, having both an "active and evolving" role, marketers call him a "prosumer" (Antéblian et al., 2013; Lipkin, 2016). In the dominant service logic (Hollebeek et al., 2014), he is perceived as a creative, contributor or integrator of operational resources.[3] His role and behaviours will engage him further with the brand. The prosumer's talents and knowledge can co-create or create value (Michaud-Trévinal, 2011). Technology has contributed to the prosumer's empowerment; it is one of the most visible forces shaping the landscape of services, such as augmented reality, mobile apps or social media. For instance, it elevated the customer at any brand's level and gave him more autonomy and control over his actions and decisions. The "sharing economy" gave birth to new forms of services such as Airbnb and Uber, where the service company no longer even exists in the traditional sense. An individual now shares his know-how and uses his knowledge to participate in the proposed offering. In a sharing economy, acquisition shifts from sustainable to ephemeral, from buying to leasing and from owning to accessing (Pomodoro, 2013). Prosumers are more informed and empowered individuals than ever.

Marketers are faced with individuals who want to consume what they want, how they want, when and where they want. They don't behave according to what a traditional consumer has been defined[4]; they are confronting "non-consumers" (Decrop, 2008). For postmodern individuals the relationship to consumption and urgency to consume is dichotomous and increasingly paradoxical. To explain this opposition, management researchers have drawn inspiration from the "Kairos/Kronos" paradox about the articulation of people's lives over time.[5] On the one hand, Kairos refers to "slow, zen or self-made". Having lost the know-how with "sedentarization" and dematerialization, individuals have had a desire to control and trace their consumer choices, to assert their civic consciousness and to move towards more qualitative choices. On the other hand, Kronos refers to getting access to "everything and immediately". The postmodern individual is thirstier to save time, to do everything and to achieve everything simultaneously. The pressure of time has also driven today's consumer into an event culture and an ephemeral culture. At a retail level, ephemeral stores are one example of temporary actions catering to postmodern consumers.

Another relationship between consumers and time refers to leisurely consumers. Loafers create "space where they can linger at the moment, at least temporarily suspend the press to reduce the productivity of their day" (Thompson & Arsel, 2004). They want to be in public while maintaining anonymity and detachment. These consumers enjoy social gatherings, the crowds and informal exchanges that enhance their experiences. Postmodern consumers, or non-consumers, are attached while remaining distant to the situations in which they are and to the people around them. They can control time by spreading it out or speeding it up. They enjoy being in public and around an audience while maintaining a detachment and maintaining superficial exchanges. Locations or spaces in which the individual allocates their time will be devoted to constructing their partial or entire experience. The place becomes time; it allows the individual to appropriate, construct or create his experience.

Postmodern consumers and their relationship with time

Postmodern consumers are becoming more sceptical and critical and less influenced by branded messages (Pan et al., 2012). Indeed, they challenge demands and habits deriving from hierarchical structures (Gransby, 1988). Always on the move, these consumers are prompted by the desire to live "portions" of experiences, or even temporary and exciting experiences. For these consumers, the importance of all action and choice emphasizes a euphoric present time and a strong denial of any concern for the future (Pomodoro, 2013); they seek immediate and urgent gratification.

> The postmodern ethic is that of carpe diem[6]: "Consume without delay, travel, have fun, do not give up anything".
> (Lipovetsky, 2004, p. 37)

As the modern consumer no longer reacts to brand proposals in a formatted way, the latter modifies their offering and retail conceptualization. Today's physical stores seem more like meeting places that individuals, residents, neighbours and friends enjoy. This strongly apparent spatio-temporal function of the store reminds one of rural business characteristics (Páramo Morales & Ramírez Plazas, 2010), where going to the store is leisure, an opportunity to meet others and spend time socializing.

An individual's relationship with time presents a tension between what he wishes to receive in exchange for the amount of time he has available (Guillard, 2017). Although the arguments presented in the past compared a consumer's "time-cost of buying" (Messinger & Narasimhan, 1997) when visiting a point of sale, it is less likely to follow this reductive formula today. Besides, commercial locations have also undergone significant changes. They have become "protean" places (Michaud-Trévinal, 2011), allowing individuals to move between traditional physical spaces, virtual spaces or transitory spaces, such as ephemeral stores. In addition to the multitude of places, the consumer is equipped with his mobile phone, smartphone, connected watch or other miniaturized tools, making it easier to access and exit any point of contact with the brand (Anteblian, 2002). The digital retail age allows customers to get in touch with brands whenever they are willing to/or want to interact. For this, they must build an ecosystem and organize it around consumption and consumer's lived reality, to be relevant to their expectation and their habits: this is the "zero moment of truth" (Reinartz & Imschloß, 2017).

At the heart of the principle of an ephemeral store's concept lies the variable of temporality; since its lifespan is very reduced, and any subsequent experience that an individual has with that store will be fleeting. The culture of "transience and immediacy" (Pomodoro, 2013) is embodied in many social consumption trends, especially the shift from ownership to sharing or renting. Customers will have pleasant experiences when they are free and freed from any bundle of obligations. The concept of ephemerality has also allowed consumers to encounter momentarily and "on the go" brands (Lowe et al., 2018). These brands appear with product proposals at the right time, in the right place and with innovative support that allows individuals to live interactive, but above all succinct, brand experiences. They are constantly seeking to conquer an individual's mental space to "position themselves firmly in the set of perceived alternatives" (Alexander, 2002).

Academic literature has been devoted to studying consumer behaviour and their store format choices. Studies have also looked at particular temporal and spatial aspects of shopping in terms of distance or accessibility (Teller et al., 2012), attractiveness and their perception as "meeting or one stop" places. Researchers have also studied their effects on consumers' emotional or behavioural reactions (Pecoraro & Usitalo, 2014). With the advent of the internet and explosion of online shopping, debates around the survival of the physical store concluded that digital and the physical retail will only be complementary and not competitive.

It has become clearer that consumers engage differently with a brand's different points of contact: physical, virtual or temporary. To better contribute to consumer expectations, brands are thinking more of presenting engaging physical and virtual channels in which "spectators" will come to attend (Pecoraro & Usitalo, 2014). This engagement is not limited to the direct relationship between the consumer and the brand; the omnipresence of social networks (Okazaki, 2009; Grewal et al., 2017), such as Facebook, Instagram, TikTok or Snapchat, reinforces the desire of internet users (or connected consumers) to engage with their extended social network and permanently access and exchange information.

The notion of time seems to evolve. Time is a variable that postmodern consumers can control to live "at the moment" on the one hand and "not worry about tomorrow" on the other. This presents a distortion of time variable's perception and the loss of contact with a time-related objective reality (Arnold & Reynolds, 2003). The perception of consumption, for instance, is changing. The life cycles of some products are becoming shorter (Davidson et al., 1976), while others may expand. More recently, discussions around sustainable consumption, sustainable economy (Baxter, 1996) or "slow[7]consumption" became frequent however does not replace "fast" related concepts: fast-fashion, fast-food or others.

While most retail activities are compared to cyclical activities (Varley, 2014), the internet has added another notion of time: "flat" time. Ubiquity and access to anyone, anytime, is becoming the new standard in the consumer world that challenges any pace to which the retail world was used. This "linear view of time" recalls a non-Western, Judeo-Christian philosophy (Brown, 1990) appealing to the "arrow of time". A consumer's relationship with time is therefore different from the exploitation of time across a given context or space ("spatio-temporal practices" can influence and transform consumer experiences). This is the case with "differential spaces" (Overdiek, 2017) that can have a transformational influence on users and surrounding spatial practices. The so-called transient environments produce an attachment to rapid renewals, to the continuous and constant desire to own new objects to admire and momentarily consume (Sachdeva & Goel, 2015). As a result, mobility, liquidity and transience generate an obsession with novelty; thus, only the "plenitude of choice" can satisfy consumers who are hungry for instant consumption.

Consumers value time based on their expectations (Binkley & Chen, 2016) of any experience they want to gain. It has been suggested that the consumer becomes less and less patient and more and more unfaithful (Pan et al., 2012). There is even talk of a "polygamous loyalty" of consumers allocating pieces of their loyalty to different brands. The complexity relating to the time dimension and the consumer's experience with a point of contact (physical or virtual) of a brand deserves our attention.

In a physical point of contact, represented by a traditional point of sale or an ephemeral point of sale, atmospheric layout investments and information affect the consumer's relationship with the time and how he will be allocating it. In a "third place" (Clauzel & Riché, 2013), a consumer creates and maintains links with the environment and with the staff present. They tend to build more personal or even family relationships which encourage him to spread out and plasticize the time to spend.

The "spatial interaction theory" emphasizes the importance of a point of sale's location touchpoint. Although most research stipulates that a consumer frequents the nearest centre offering the required good or service, the theory of spatial interaction assumes that he will also be able to go in search of places that may present alternatives that meet his desires, needs or expectations (Brown, 1993). The consumer will trade the time it takes to get to a given place with the satisfaction that he can derive from such a transaction. Several studies have variously examined the temporal orientation of the consumer, the pressure exerted on the consumer by fragmented time and the effect of such fragmentation on the processing of information by the consumer (De Lassus & Freire, 2014).

The issue of time allocation is of major importance in the context of multichannel or omnichannel retailing, as consumers will be able to divide their time between research, time spent and purchase and navigation between the various points of contact presented by the brand. This depends on consumer motivations and whether they are hasty (Vanheems, 2012) or if they have more time available. Time availability (Beatty & Ferrell, 1998) is considered as an "exogenous variable" which influences the length of time the consumer will stay in a point of sale, more particularly his discretionary use of time navigation.

Numerous atmospheric indices influence the nature of consumers' "time spent" (Ballantine et al., 2016). Whether it is to buy, to browse, to stroll or to explore, the time spent is a significant result in consumer behaviour. It may be "monochronic" (Welté & Ochs, 2005) or may correspond to a phased breakdown of a consumer's journey. A store's atmosphere also influences consumers' willingness to research or explore (Turley & Milliman, 2000). And finally, the time spent is a result of the consumer's immersion in an experience. The more multi-sensory and immersive this experience, the more the consumer is likely to increase the time spent in a point of sale (Foster & McLelland, 2014). Ephemeral stores, for instance, are characterized by their limited lifespans and can lead to "time pressure". They are considered a time dimension of the consumption experience (De Lassus, 2012). Indeed, the spatio-temporal dimension of the experience is one of the four dimensions which is added to the sensory, emotional and aesthetic dimensions (Lemon, & Verhoef, 2016).

In search of meanings

Previous studies[8] have emphasized the importance of market relationships and the symbolic, even religious (Turner, 1966), appropriation of consumption. With the advent of discretionary income in industrialized country households, "ostentatious consumption" appears. This type of consumption characterizes the ability to "spend without counting" and without having to deprive yourself of any essentials (Langlois, 2002). On the other hand, the "voluntary dispossession of goods by the consumer" (Lemaitre & De Barnier, 2015) thinks of consuming differently,[9] better and by acknowledging the value of consumed goods (Bryant & Goodman, 2004). Although possession remains one of the reasons for consumption, an individual seeks more the meaning acquired through the act of consumption. As consumers no longer merely buy products, they go in the direction of self-expression and the identification of the relationships built through consumption (Sachdeva & Goel, 2015); and therefore, the consumer not only buys for "what he can do" with the product but also for "what it wants to say" when buying it (Hirschman & Holbrook, 1982).

> But while art proper claims its proud sovereignty in contempt for money and hatred of the bourgeois world, "a commercial art" is constituted which, turned towards the search for profit, immediate and temporary success, tends to become an economic world like any other by adapting to the demands of

the public and by offering "risk-free" products that are rapidly obsolete.

(Lipovetsky & Serroy, 2013)

Through consumption, the individual "enables non-verbal communication" and achieves the satisfaction of self-expression (Belk et al., 1982). In addition to the act of buying, consumers are looking for "hedonic consumption" which refers to facets of behaviour that relate to the "multi-sensory, fantastic and emotional" aspects of their experience with the products. The consumer, therefore, seeks to allocate his expenses to live "exceptional experiences" (Sachdeva & Goel, 2015) instead of simple acts of purchase. He has the tendency to consume "spirituality"[10] and search for meaning or well-being. Consumption can therefore be considered as a reason for expression or acquisition and integration of the object's meanings that the consumer acquires (Camus & Poulain, 2008; Poulain et al., 2013).

Moreover, consumption is a religion in its own right; it has its symbols and its rites. Being part of this religion implies respecting a set of beliefs and codes specific to a given school of thought. Consumption fills a void from which the consumer suffers and he has prescribed a cure. A ritual is defined as "a formally prescribed conduct linked to belief in beings or mystical forces" (Páramo Morales & Ramírez Plazas, 2010) (Deflem, 1991). It is therefore, through rituals, that a person asserts himself within his social group (Bô, 2013), just as he witnesses symbolic collective acts that unite group members, and contribute to constructing their identity. In the physical context, engagement occurs through the activation of the individual's senses, while in an online store the experience is not quite the same as it is mostly limited to two-dimensional images and text. Once at the point of sale, the consumer seeks to "experience pleasure" (Monglo, 2016) which can be reduced to the purchase itself or to the time spent on research (Binkley & Chen, 2016). The distinction between shopping as "work" and shopping as "leisure" (Woodruffe-Burton, 2001) is still blurred. Consumers' pleasure-related experiences may be the sole focus of the point-of-sale's visit as they may be permitted within a chore shopping sequence (Anteblian, 2002).

A consumer's "desire" is a type of imaginative process, a passion born between his fantasies and the situational social contexts in which he lives. Past research has insisted that technology slows down customer desires because it is linked to an increase in rationality and that "human/software" interaction sites transform customer desire into a "task-oriented" practice. The human-technology relationship might thus transform the experience of an enjoyable pursuit to a more functional and goal-oriented task (Kozinets et al., 2017). But consumers are increasingly demanding memorable (Klein et al., 2016), extravagant and disproportionate and experiences (De Lassus & Freire, 2014). In fact, today's shopping experiences involve educational, event-based and entertainment experiences (Fiore & Kim, 2007). In addition to memorable experiences, consumers also expect to be provided with engaging experiences (Niehm et al., 2007). These engaged consumers also want products, communications, entertainment and marketing efforts that sting their senses, evoke emotions and stimulate their thinking; they expect and respond better to experiences and want shopping to be fun. With ephemeral stores, brands can foster unique and sensational experiences that appeal to the growing desire for innovation and openness towards diverse and unique experiences (Kim et al., 2010).

Retailers have recently turned to propose theatrical places, re-enchanting and leading to the creation of highly thematic environments (Antéblian et al., 2013). It is in these sacred "consumption habitats" that consumers can spend a "sacred time" (Woodruffe-Burton, 2001). A point of sale's atmosphere (or a point of contact) becomes a "psychological" comfort tool (Ainsworth & Ballantine, 2014), allowing consumers a significant reduction in the complexity that they may face during a traditional purchasing situation. Pop-up stores often change the symbolic order of a store. They are not usually designed to sell but to immerse users in shared experiences. To provide an experience in these stores, it will be necessary to understand customer preferences, as well as to co-develop new meanings for their brands' propositions. In many cases, consumers visiting a pop-up store are seen as active agents who seek to co-create their experience (Overdiek, 2017).

Informed, engaged and involved; how consumers are influencing retail's evolution

Consumers' prior knowledge and assessments are defined as "the amount of specific information held in memory as well as the self-perceived knowledge" (Gauzente, 2010). A consumer's prior knowledge has both advantages and disadvantages. Among the advantages are higher categorization abilities, the use of more subtle perceptual factors in discrimination tasks and reduced problem recognition time. The main drawback is linked to the phenomenon of the feeling of knowing, which introduces a bias into decision-making processes.

Information is a significant factor in the customer decision-making process. The more informed he is, the more he becomes an expert and will be able to transmit knowledge, will have a higher level of know-how and will control or master his experience. The internet and technology allow him to make more informed decisions about which products or services to consume (Grewal et al., 2017), by highlighting textual and visual presentations and by sharing descriptive or technical information of the proposed offer. The consumer (or internet user) becomes endowed with digital capacities (well-informed, digitally enabled), becomes more of an expert and more informed (Gallen & Cases, 2007). He seeks elements of differentiation (Welté & Ochs, 2005), thus creating a new electronic (Anderson et al., 2011) and physical retail ecosystem. Flawless management between physical and digital environments (omnichannel contexts) becomes more important as it takes into account a more confident, more secure consumer who navigates different brand channels (Bernon et al., 2016).

Customers are also looking for building meaningful relationships with brands. Immersion is one of the key elements (Petermans et al., 2013) of consumer-brand engagement and can be explained in retail contexts as being fully engrossed in the task of purchase (Foster & McLelland, 2014). It is, in fact, the result of a process comprising back and forth and "rarely instantaneous" and "frequently partial" (Simon, 2008). Focusing on a research goal and the attention resources granted help maintain sustained immersion throughout the activity. Therefore, the perception of cognitive control over the activity is likely to induce a hedonic sensation constituting a customer's experience (in stores and on the internet).

Changes in consumer preferences (Gallouj & Gallouj, 2009) also play an important role in the emergence and development of new sales formulas. Today's brands are faced with active, participatory and creative consumers (Salerno, 2009); their roles go beyond that of passive recipients (Slywotzky et al., 2000). For most of the 20th century, customers were "product and price takers", accepting goods without discussion or revolt. Customers have become more sophisticated over the last decades and have gained more power over the buying process and are armed with more options and information. They are involved with brands on several levels; in physical, virtual or ephemeral points of sale and on social networks (Hollebeek et al., 2014). They want to apply their own rules of consumption anywhere, anytime, at their own pace or in an appropriated place. They want to shop online, offline, from their computers or their smartphones. And they are more than ever at outlets that facilitate their shopping experiences and that meet their expectations (which are varied and that can vary all times).

The retail environment has been put to a great test and has led brands to rethink their retail strategies, the choice of distribution channels or the operationalization of these channels. Traditional retail rules have become less relevant and consequently pushed brands to act upon what seems pertinent to the business and what can keep it running in a healthy way. Different brand types, operating at different market levels and in different industries, will probably select retail channels that are easily managed and that don't handicap the brand's operations. Brands will not conform to "what should be done"; rather, they will be "doing what they do best and in the best ways possible".

It is pretentious to forecast the future of retail or to predict retail format evolution or growth. What seems more possible and looks plausible is a "meets-end" strategy, looking at what the brand has, enhancing it to best meet customer needs at the right time and in the right moment. To add on retail environmental uncertainties, customers are behaving in unpredictable patterns, and are becoming more sophisticated, more demanding and less loyal. They surf online, spend time offline, and switch their patterns and preferences without prior warning. If today's brands want to remain relevant, they have to be a step ahead of their target audiences and have to carefully choose channels through which they operate to provide a seamless (and flawless) omnichannel experience.

What are the possibilities for ephemeral retail revolution and evolution? "Time" is today's currency (Lloyd Wallis, 2020) perfectly reflecting customers that act upon the moment and care about instant gratification. Time also relates to what happens on the spot, and coincides right in front of the customer just when he needs it. Whether offline or online, brands who get in touch with customers at that right moment are those who will gain their attention and (maybe their eventual) confidence. Ephemeral retail will be the brand's application to actions seeking to meet customer needs and in the most relevant way possible: online, in a store, on the road, in a park through a video call or a chat, and with respect to prevailing environmental situations. Who thought of purchasing fried chicken through a fully automated car (Entrepreneur, 2020)? It is through this invaluable time currency that brands provide momentary occasions allowing customers to make the most of their divided time; adding value to it. So, it is "now or never" for brands. Either they meet up with their customers here and now, or they have to look for another available opportunity before manifesting before them.

Ephemeral retail helps brands turn uncertainties into opportunities (Retail Doctor Group., 2020). This agile, *sur-mesure*, format offers brands the possibility to gather all elements that create value and deliver it at the right time to the right target audience. Physical ephemeral stores present unique, innovative concepts allowing customers to activate their senses, draw their journey and live unique experiences. Online ephemeral stores stretch the brand's reach beyond a physical point to meet audiences virtually and to increase the possibilities of interacting with the brand. The digitalization of physical ephemeral stores intensifies the customer offline/online journey to create more value and craft a sense of uniqueness in his heart and mind. Retail is going back to being simple and looking at simple ways of getting in touch with customers. Even if today's retail might involve state-of-the-art digital tools, it does not mean that it becomes complex and complicated. By "simple" we mean that retail is looking at simplifying the user experience to the extent that it becomes as natural as the individual/customer's daily activity.

Today's ephemeral retail is not new; it is simply adding value and giving more meaning to the retail scene. It breaks monotony and animates, it refreshes, it energises and it revitalises. It reflects a brand's identity and meets its needs with upmost simplicity; it meets customers naturally, without complications and moves on. Through ephemeral stores, brands humanize further their identity and stay in contact with customers by coping up with their agenda, activities and gatherings to meaningfully present something new. Ephemeral retail can be physical or digital and can be recurrent or accidental. At times when retail and distribution channels have witnessed difficulties, ephemeral retail injected a sense of novelty by giving a different meaning to what distribution and communications could look like and could mean.

A new era or new retail horizons?

Notes

1 As stated by Lipovetsky (1990) (Badot et al., 2018)
2 "Positive or negative" emotions and the appropriation of "real and virtual" spaces.

3 Consumer innovativeness refers to the one who has a general or specific personality trait linked to a particular field (Fowler & Bridges, 2010). This consumer has a predisposition to discover and adopt new products in a specific field and therefore implies that consumers' "innovativeness" is not often transmitted between different consumer products.

4 "Strictly speaking, the consumer is the person using or consuming the product. The consumer is not necessarily the buyer or the decision-maker. Taking this state of affairs into account is sometimes very important for marketing decision-making" (www.definitions-marketing.com)

5 *"Kairos refers to the right time of the moment turned into action while Kronos refers to the measurable and linearly flowing time"* (Decrop, 2008).

6 Enjoying and taking advantage of the present moment: An expression taken from the verses of Horace, a Roman philosopher of Antiquity: *"Carpe diem, quam minimum credula postero"*, which means "seize the day without worrying about the next day, and be less gullible for the next day" (www.linternaute.fr).

7 The "slow" trend in interior decoration or interior furniture, for example (https://lilm.co/inspiration/astuces/slow-furniture-meubles/)

8 Studies in anthropology as in sociology have been interested in "the consumption of objects around the concepts of exchange, symbolic appropriation and objectification" (Langlois, 2002) as suggested by Veblen (1899) and Miller (1995).

9 We are referring to "alternative" consumption (Bryant & Goodman, 2004).

10 The theme of spirituality has been the subject of a limited number of publications in the field of marketing research, particularly in France. It is directly addressed through the field of value. Badot and Cova (1992) had already underlined this axis of evolution in a more "macro" way by speaking of the return of meaning in the markets (Poulain et al., 2013).

References

Ainsworth, J. & Ballantine, P. W., 2014. That's different! How consumers respond to retail website change. *Journal of Retailing and Consumer Services*, 21, pp. 764–772.

Alexander, A., 2002. Retailing and consumption: Evidence from war time Britain. *International Review of Retail, Distribution and Consumer Research*, 12(1), pp. 39–57.

Anderson, M., Buckner, N. & Eikelmann, S., 2011. The M-Commerce challenge to retail. *Strategy + Business*, 62, pp. 1–5.

Anteblian, B., 2002. *Le consommateur et le déplacement au point de vente*. s.l.: 5ème colloque Etienne THIL.

Antéblian, B., Filser, M. & Roederer, C., 2013. L'expérience du consommateur dans le commerce de détail. Une revue de littérature. *Recherche et Applications en Marketing*, 28(3), pp. 84–114.

Arnold, M. J. & Reynolds, K. E., 2003. Hedonic shopping motivations. *Journal of Retailing*, 79, pp. 77–95.

Badot, O., Lemoine, J.-F. & Ochs, A., 2018. *Distribution 4.0.* 1st ed. s.l.: Pearson.

Ballantine, P., Parsons, A. & Comeskey, K., 2016. A conceptual model of the holistic effects of atmospheric cues in fashion retailing. *International Journal of Retail & Distribution Management*, 43(6), pp. 503–517.

Baxter, M., 1996. Are consumer durables important for business cycles? *The Review of Economics and Statistics*, February, 78(1), pp. 147–155.

Beatty, S. E. & Ferrell, E., 1998. Impulse buying: Modeling its precursors. *Journal of Retailing*, 74(2), pp. 169–191.

Belk, R. W., Bahn, K. D. & Mayer, R. N., 1982. Developmental recognition of consumption symbolism. *The Journal of Consumer Research*, June, 9(1), pp. 4–17.

Bernon, M., Cullen, J. & Gorst, J., 2016. Online retail returns management. Integration within an omni-channel distribution context. *International Journal of Physical Distribution & Logistics Management*, 46(6/7), pp. 584–605.

Binkley, J. K. & Chen, S. E., 2016. Consumer shopping strategies and prices paid in retail food markets. *The Journal of Consumer Affairs*, 50(3), pp. 557–584.

Bô, D., 2013. *Brand culture. Développer le potentiel culturel de la marque.* Paris: Dunod.

Brown, S., 1990. The wheel of retailing: Past and future. *Journal of Retailing*, Summer, 66(2), pp. 143–149.

Brown, S., 1993. Retail location theory: Evolution and evaluation. *International Review of Retail, Distribution & Consumer Research*, 3(2), pp. 186–229.

Bryant, R. L. & Goodman, M. K., 2004. Consuming narratives: The political ecology of « alternative » consumption. *Transactions of the Institute of British Geographers*, 29(3), pp. 344–366.

Camus, S. & Poulain, M., 2008. La spiritualité: émergence d'une tendance dans la consommation. *Management & Avenir*, 5(19), pp. 72–90.

Chen, W.-C. & Fiore, A. M., 2017. Factors affecting Taiwanese consumers' responses toward pop-up retail. *Asia Pacific Journal of Marketing and Logistics*, 29(2), pp. 370–392.

Clauzel, A. & Riché, C., 2013. Relation-client et gestion du temps de consommation: quel rôle du sourire du personnel en contact en restauration? *Revue Française du Marketing*, 4/5(244/245), pp. 244/245.

Davidson, W. R., Bates, A. D. & Bass, S. J., 1976. The retail life cycle. *Harvard Business Review*, pp. 89–96.

Decrop, A., 2008. Les paradoxes du consommateur postmoderne. *Reflets et Perspectives de la Vie Economique*, 2(Tome XLVII), pp. 85–93.

Deflem, M., 1991. Ritual, anti-structure, and religion: A discussion of victor turner's processual symbolic analysis. *Journal for the Scientific Study of Religion*, 30(1), pp. 1–25.

De Lassus, C., 2012. Les pop-up stores de luxe entre lieu mythique et endroit éphémère, une analyse sémiotique. *Colloque Etienne Thil*, Paris, France, Oct.

De Lassus, C. & Freire, A., 2014. Acess to luxury brand myth in pop-up stores: A netnographic and semiotic analysis. *Journal of Retailing and Customer Services*, 21, pp. 61–68.

Entrepreneur, 2020. KFC turned to self-driving cars in China to deliver fried chicken while limiting human contact. [Online] Available at https://www.entrepreneur.com/article/360486 [Accessed 27 11 2020].

Fiore, A. and Kim, J., 2007. An interactive framework capturing experiential shopping experience. *International Journal of Retail and Distribution Management*. 35(6), pp. 421–442.

Foster, J. & McLelland, M. A., 2014. Retail atmospherics: The impact of a brand dictated theme. *Journal of Retailing and Consumer Services*, 22, pp. 195–205.

Fowler, K. & Bridges, E., 2010. Consumer innovativeness: Impact on expectations, perceptions, and choice among retail formats. *Journal of Retailing and Consumer Services*, 17, pp. 492–500.

Gallen, C. & Cases, A.-S., 2007. Le rôle du risque perçu et de l'expérience dans l'achat de vin en ligne. *Décision Marketing*, (45), pp. 58–74.

Gauzente, C., 2010. The intention to click on sponsored ads—A study of the role of prior knowledge and of consumer profile. *Journal of Retailing and Consumer Services*, 17, pp. 457–463.

Gransby, D. M., 1988. The coexistence of high street and out-of-town retailing from a retailing perspective. *The Geographical Journal*, March, 151(1), pp. 13–16.

Grewal, D., Roggeveen, A. L. & Nordfält, J., 2017. The Future of Retailing. 91(1), pp. 1–6.

Guillard, V., 2017. Comprendre la relation collaborative d'échange de temps au sein des Accorderies. Une analyse par la théorie de l'échange social. *Revue Française De Gestion*, 43(265), pp. 9–23.

Hagberg, J., Sundstrom, M. & Egels-Zandén, N., 2016. The digitalization of retailing: An exploratory framework. *International Journal of Retail & Distribution Management*, 44(7), pp. 694–712.

Hirschman, E. C. & Holbrook, M. B., 1982. Hedonic consumption: Emerging concepts, methods and propositions. *Journal of Marketing*, Summer, 46(3), pp. 92–101.

Hollebeek, L. D., Glynn, M. S. & Brodie, R. J., 2014. Consumer brand engagement in social media: Conceptualization, scale development and validation. *Journal of Interactive Marketing*, 28, pp. 149–165.

Kim, H., Fiore, A., Niehm, L. & Jeong, M., 2010. Psychographic characteristics affecting behavioral intentions towards pop-up retail. *International Journal of Retail & Distribution Management*, 38(2), pp. 133–154.

Klein, J. F., Falk, T., Esch, F.-R. & Gloukhovtsev, A., 2016. Linking pop-up brand stores to brand experience and word of mouth: The case of luxury retail. *Journal of Business Research*, 69(12), pp. 5761–5767.

Kozinets, R., Patterson, A. & Ashman, R., 2017. Networks of desire: How technology increases our passion to consume. *Journal of Consumer Research*, 43, pp. 659–682.

Langlois, S., 2002. Nouvelles orientations en sociologie de la consommation. *L'année Sociologique*, 1(52), pp. 83–103.

Lemaitre, N. & De Barnier, V., 2015. Quand le consommateur devient commerçant: motivations, production d'expérience et perspectives. *Décisions Marketing*, (78), pp. 11–28.

Lemon, K. N. & Verhoef, P. C., 2016. Understanding customer experience throughout the customer journey. *Journal of Marketing: AMA/MSI Special Issue*, 80, pp. 69–96.

Lipkin, M., 2016. Customer experience formation in today's service landscape. *Journal of Service Management*, 27(5), pp. 678–703.

Lipovetsky, G., 2004. *Les temps hypermodernes*. Paris: Grasset.

Lipovetsky, G. & Serroy, J., 2013. *L'esthétisation du monde vivre à l'âge du capitalisme artiste*. 1–22 ed. Gallimard (Version extrait electronique): s.n.

Lloyd Wallis, A., 2020. Consumer and retailer sentiment. Retail Doctor Group, p. 25.

Marciniak, R. & Budnarowska, C., 2018. *Exploration of pop-up retail: The department store perspective*. Belgium, 4th International colloquium on design, branding and marketing (ICDBM).

Messinger, P. R. & Narasimhan, C., 1997. A model of retail formats based on consumers' economizing on shopping time. *Marketing Science*, 16(1), pp. 1–23.

Michaud-Trévinal, A., 2011. Expérience de magasinage et appropriation des espaces commerciaux. *Management & Avenir*, 7(47), pp. 240–259.

Monglo, H., 2016. L'influence du comportement de butinage sur une conséquence transactionnelle au point de vente: une application à l'achat non planifié en supermarché au Cameroun. *Revue Management & Avenir*, 84, pp. 15–29.

Niehm, L. S., Ann Marie, F., Jeong, M. & Kim, H.-J., 2007. Pop-up Retail's Acceptability as an Innovative Business Strategy and Enhancer of the Consumer Shopping Experience. *Journal of Shopping Center Research*, 13(7), pp. 1–30.

Okazaki, S., 2009. The tactical use of mobile marketing: How adolescents' social networking can best shape brand extentions. *Journal of Advertising Research*, 49(1), pp. 12–26.

Overdiek, A., 2017. Fashionable interventions: The pop-up store as a differential space. *Organizational Aesthetics*, 6(1), pp. 116–134.

Pan, Y., Sheng, S. & Xie, F. T., 2012. Antecedents of customer loyalty: An empirical synthesis and reexamination. *Journal of Retailing and Consumer Services*, 19, pp. 150–158.

Páramo Morales, D. & Ramírez Plazas, E., 2010. Significaciones rituales asociadas a la labor de los tenderos de barrio. *Pensamiento y gestión*, 28, pp. 196–216.

Pecoraro, M. & Usitalo, O., 2014. Exploring the everyday retail experience: The discourses of style and design. *Journal of Consumer Behaviour*, 13, pp. 429–441.

Petermans, A., Janssens, W. & Van Cleempoel, K., 2013. A holistic framework for conceptualizing customer experiences in retail environments. *International Journal of Design*, 7(2), pp. 1–18.

Picot-Coupey, K., 2012. Pop-up stores and the international development of retail networks. *11 International Marketing Trends Conference*, Venezia, Jan.

Piotrowicz, W. & Cuthbertson, R., 2014. Introduction to the special issue information technology in retail: Toward omnichannel retailing. *International Journal of Electronic Commerce*, 18(4), pp. 5–15.

Pomodoro, S., 2013. Temporary retail in fashion system: An explorative study. *Journal of Fashion Marketing and Management: An International Journal*, 17(3), pp. 341–352.

Poulain, M., Badot, O. & Camus, S., 2013. La spiritualité dans l'expérience de magasinage. Cadre théorique et exploration empirique. *Revue Interdisciplinaire Management, Homme & Entreprise*, 4(8), pp. 40–46.

Reinartz, W. & Imschloß, M., 2017. From point of sale to point of need: How digital technology is transforming retailing. *The Future of Retailing*, 9(1).

Retail Doctor Group., 2020. Global retail innovations during Covid-19. Retail Doctor Group, p. 109.

Rieunier, S. & Volle, P., 2002. Tendances de consommation et stratégies de différenciation des distributeurs. *Décisions Marketing*, 27, pp. 19–30.

Russo Spena, T., Caridà, A., Colurcio, M. & Melia, M., 2012. Store experience and co-creation: The case of temporary shop. *International Journal of Retail & Distribution Management*, 40(1), pp. 21–40.

Sachdeva, I. & Goel, S., 2015. Retail store environement and customer experience: A paradigm. *Journal of Fashion Marketing Management*, 19(3), pp. 290–298.

Simon, F., 2008. Intensité de la recherche d'information et expérience de consommation sur Internet: le cas d'une primo-visite pour l'achat d'un cadeau. *Systèmes d'information & management*, 1(13), pp. 63–88.

Slywotzky, A., Christensen, C. M., Tedlow, R. S. & Carr, N. G., 2000. The future of commerce. *Harvard Business Review*, pp. 1–20.

Teller, C., Kotzab, H. & Grant, D. B., 2012. The relevance of shopper logistics for consumers of store-based retail formats. *Journal of Retailing and Consumer Services*, 19, pp. 59–66.

Thompson, C. & Arsel, Z., 2004. The Starbucks brandscape and consumers' (anticorporate) experiences of glocalization. *Journal of Consumer Research*, 31, pp. 31–642.

Turley, L. W. & Milliman, R. E., 2000. Atmospheric effects on shopping behavior: A review of the experimental evidence. *Journal of Business Research*, 49, pp. 193–211.

Turner, V., 1966. The ritual process. Structure and anti-structure. *Cornell Paperbacks. Cornell University Press*, p. 213.

Vanheems, R., 2012. Multicanalisation des enseignes. Comment internet transforme les comportements en magasin. *Revue Française de Gestion*, 8(227), pp. 13–29.

Varley, R., 2014. Selecting products in: Retail product management. *Routledge*, pp. 57–75.

Veblen, T., 1899. *The theory of the leisure class.* New York, NY: Macmillan.

Welté, J.-B. & Ochs, L., 2005. Une analyse de la crise de l'hypermarché par un objet symbole: le caddie. *Ethnologie française*, 35(1), pp. 81–91.

Woodruffe-Burton, H., 2001. Towards a theory of shopping: A holistic framework. *Journal of Consumer Behavior*, 1(3), pp. 256–266.

Index

agile 18, 23, 40, 126
agility 3, 40
"AirBnB" 35, 116
artistic dimension 49
atmospheric dimensions 6; indices
    120; layout 120; stores 13;
    variables 13
attitudes 4, 7, 17, 70

behavioural intentions 2, 7, 71;
    reactions 118
brand identity 23, 27, 126
brand objectives 39
brand strategy 40
buzz 2, 40, 48, 50, 61, 64–66

cognitive engagement 73
cognitive level 63
"community store" 4
customer behaviour 6, 61, 98,
    114, 118
customer-centric 39, 61, 104
customer emotions 5, 6, 13, 126
customer experience 61; engaging
    123; memorable 16; sensational
    123; unique 20, 123

desire 10, 16, 43, 59, 70, 96, 113,
    114, 116–117, 120, 122–123
"digital divide" 26
digitalization 59, 72, 89
disruption 83, 84, 86–87, 93, 99–103
distribution channel 8, 48, 59,
    89–90, 95
dwellers 18

e-commerce 59, 72, 92, 94
emotional dimension 61

engaging 16, 22, 25, 50, 58, 64–65,
    73, 119, 123
England 84, 86
environmental psychology 114
evolution 84; evolutionary 84
exclusivity 28, 38, 49, 64–65, 114
experience 5, 11, 13–16, 49, 61–64,
    66–67, 69, 88, 105, 113–114,
    117–118, 122–123
experiential dimension 49, 67
experiential marketing 7, 10, 12–14,
    26, 39, 49, 64, 68–69
"extraordinary brand experience" 50

fashion 2, 18; fashion week 1; cycles
    60 retailers 2
flexibility 39, 40, 49–50, 65, 103
formats: multi-line; 58; self-service
    58; traditional 58

globalized retail market 72
guerrilla marketing 64–65

hedonic benefits 69–70, 114
holistic 4, 14
hyper-real 112–113; hyper-engaged
    96; hypermodern 50, 60, 113
hyper-retail 44

industry 11, 85–87, 89
innovation 79
innovative 1, 24, 37, 40, 64, 118;
    alternatives 36; business strategy
    3; concepts 1, 68, 126; consumers
    67; experience 44; formats
    42–43, 60; merchandising 30;
    people 70; solutions 48–49, 97;
    tool 63

interaction 2, 49, 61, 64, 70, 73, 89, 95, 99–100, 122; experiential 64; social 70
interactive environment 49–50; place 62
interactive experiences 14; performances 67
interactive platform 48
internet 20, 22, 24, 37, 44, 49, 58, 61, 87, 90–97, 100, 102, 118–119, 124
internet users 20, 22, 24, 37, 61, 92–93, 103, 119

landlords 28
landscape 88, 91, 116; retail 59, 87, 93; urban 38
"latest expression of innovative solutions" 48
limited: duration 49; edition 3, 19, 28, 38, 47, 72; lifespan 18, 25, 38, 43, 121; lifetime 67; time 1, 38, 47, 50
liquidity 59, 112–113, 119
location 1, 3, 5, 17–26, 38, 41, 46–47, 50, 66, 70, 83–84, 92, 100, 104, 117; relocation 92
loyalty 38, 40, 44, 46, 64, 104; polygamous loyalty 120
luxury brands 1–2, 7–8, 22, 45–46, 67, 69

marketing-mix 12–16, 65, 88, 99; communication mix 50; retail mix 83; strategic mix 45
market-mavens 68, 70, 72
metamorphosis 57, 102, 104
millennials 62, 71
mobility 40, 59–60, 112–113, 119
multi-channel 58, 90, 95–96, 97–99, 101, 120
multi-sensory 4–6, 13–14, 46, 48, 63, 68, 121–122; experience 5

omni channel strategy 72

Paris 1, 17–18
places: experiential 26; magical 26; temporary 57; unrestricted 25; vacant 25
"places to be" 2
points of contact 12, 24, 37, 46, 49, 62, 68, 93, 97, 104, 119, 120

postmodern 43, 49–50, 59–60, 62, 112–114, 116–117; postmodernity 112, 117
providers: e-commerce 59; service 29; space 25
PUIS 41

"real experiences" 59
retail disruption 83–84, 93, 99–103, 104
retail evolution 84

shopping malls 3, 58, 101
short-term 37, 44–46, 65
showrooming 61–62
smartphone 17, 27, 48, 59, 61, 93, 101, 118, 125
social commerce 93–94
"social interaction theory" 120
social media 61, 66–68, 73, 93–94, 116
social mobility 60
social networks 3, 17, 24, 50, 61–62, 66–67, 71, 73
stimuli 6, 12, 98, 112
"sustainable temporary store" 4
"Swiss army Knife" 40

technology 13, 18, 20, 26–27, 37, 42, 50, 61, 76, 80, 87–89, 93, 95, 104, 116, 122–123
technology-savvy 3, 42
temporal 120; temporality 65, 118; spatio-temporal 117, 119, 121
"temporary activations" 64
"test store" 4
theatrical 49, 64, 123
"three-dimensional piece of communication" 61
time variable 119
transient environment 59, 113, 119

utilitarian: advantages 50; beliefs 72; benefits 69–70, 114

vacant spaces 13, 28, 38, 41, 58; places 25
value: co-creation 5; creation 27, 83, 89, 94

wheel of retailing 81; distribution wheel 81, 82, 88; retail wheel 81

For Product Safety Concerns and Information please contact our
EU representative GPSR@taylorandfrancis.com Taylor & Francis
Verlag GmbH, Kaufingerstraße 24, 80331 München, Germany